## Praise for *WE ARE THE POWER*

*We Are the Power* cuts through the noise with a blunt reminder: democracy doesn't defend itself — and no one's coming to save it. In this timely and practical playbook, Gary Lucks deftly turns outrage into organization and anxiety into action. It's a much-needed instruction manual: clear, direct, and grounded in what actually works — and what's desperately needed.

— **Joel Makower**, Chairman, Trellis Group

For a clear understanding of what's at stake, and a road map that will provide you with a pathway to help save our country, there's no better place to start than Gary Lucks' *We Are the Power*. If our country and our democracy are to be saved, WE ALL will need to be part of the solution. Discover the most effective way for you to add to this incredibly important effort. We ARE the power!

— **Winston Hickox**, Past President of the Board of the
California League of Conservation Voters

After more than forty years working with Gary Lucks, one thing is clear: he never stops getting better. I've seen him excel as an advocate for protecting wild rivers, a strategist electing environmental champions, a policy adviser to legislators and a governor, a citizen organizer with Indivisible, and throughout it all, a respected environmental attorney in California. There is no better mentor to guide your way.

*We Are the Power* distills that lifetime of experience into a clear, practical playbook. The steps are simple—but not easy—and they work if you do. Follow them, and you will mobilize a force of citizens capable of standing up to authoritarianism, wherever it appears. At a time when many feel anxious and overwhelmed, Gary offers not just hope, but a roadmap. Use it, and you become part of the force that renews and protects our democracy.

— **Bill Shireman**, CEO of Solution Citizen

Other books describe the perils we face and why we should act, but this book describes what we can do to address the threats to our country. This practical guide answers the question "What can I do?" and should be in the hands of every citizen and organizer.

— **Eleanor LeCain** JD, Chairwoman, Electing Women National Democratic Region, Director of Programs, Women's National Democratic Club

Too many people are waiting for someone else to save democracy. Gary Lucks makes the compelling case — backed by data and decades of experience — that we are the cavalry we've been waiting for. *We Are the Power* is an indispensable resource for everyone who refuses to sit on the sidelines.

— **Dave Jones** JD, Insurance Commissioner of California, Emeritus

In a time characterized by panic, outrage, and despair, Gary Lucks offers a much-needed alternative -- a calm, calculated response to the question 'what can I do?' This

book is a clear 'how to' manual for saving our democracy from the grips of wannabe totalitarians."
— **Nathaniel Markowitz**, Executive Director of
Activate America

At a time when the nation's constitutional foundations are under unprecedented strain, Gary Lucks delivers a powerful reminder that democracy depends on active participation. This book equips readers, whether legally trained or not, with practical, accessible strategies to defend and strengthen our system from within."
— **Brian Copeland**, Author, activist,
Hall of Fame broadcaster.

In an era of disinformation and algorithmic outrage, Gary Lucks offers something rare: a calm, rigorous strategy for turning anxiety into action. This is not a book of talking points — it's a durable manual for sustaining a democratic movement over the long haul.
— **Darrell Steinberg**, JD, former Mayor of Sacramento
and California State Senate Leader

Gary Lucks makes a convincing case for urgent and strategic political action. He gets the reader energized to meaningfully engage in the democratic process, during 2026 and beyond. As a country, we face existential threats and Gary both invites and politely demands that we all stand together in support of our most precious democratic principles and rights. *We Are the Power* is the roadmap to the recovery of our national pride.
— **Kevin Johnson** MA, JD,
author of *The American Oath Project*

Movements burn out when they sprint without a plan. Gary Lucks draws on decades of organizing across multiple election cycles and understands the rhythm of sustained democratic action better than anyone writing today. *We Are the Power* doesn't just fire you up for November. It maps the road through 2027, 2028, and beyond. That's the kind of thinking that actually wins.

— **Doug Linney**, Founder of Activate America

In decades of public service, I've seen movements rise and fall on the quality of their organizing. Gary Lucks understands what actually moves the needle — and he's laid it out here with uncommon clarity and passion. Read this book and then get to work.

— **Heidi Sanborn,** MPH, Circular Economy Leader and Consultant

In this era of chaos and daily threats to our freedoms and the Constitution, *We Are the Power* is a guidebook for how each citizen can become active in reclaiming our democracy and setting it on the right path for generations to come. The book clearly outlines how to get involved and make a difference, whether one lives in a red, blue, or purple region of the country. Commit To Democracy agrees wholeheartedly with the book's premise that in community there is strength and that engagement in one's government is the key to a living and thriving democracy.

— **Linda Carman** and **Molly Hermes**, Co-leaders of Commit to Democracy

# WE ARE THE POWER

## To Win the Future

YOUR COUNTRY NEEDS YOU

GARY LUCKS

**Community Organizer & Attorney**

# CONTENTS

# DEDICATION

To my sister, Lisa Lucks Mendel who has always been a foundational, loving, and reliable supporter and friend and to Karen Shore--the backbone of our Indivisible Group--who brings her commitment, organization, and sanity as we navigate these turbulent times. And to my son, Dylan Lucks, who inspires me to do all I can to help ensure a bright future for him and his generation. And finally, to our many committed, creative, volunteer team who doggedly advance our mission and for whom I am so grateful.

# INTRODUCTION

# THE MOST IMPORTANT DECADE OF OUR LIFETIME

*In the face of great perils never before encountered,
our strong purpose is to protect and to perpetuate
the integrity of democracy.*
**Franklin D. Roosevelt**
32nd President of the United States

I have campaigned in every election cycle since I was in college. Every two years, in presidential elections and midterms. Win or lose. Rain or shine. I have never been more concerned about the future of our country than I am at this moment.

Let me introduce myself. I am an environmental lawyer, as well as a scientist, policy adviser, adjunct professor, and author. While I have always believed in progressive values and felt it was my civic responsibility to campaign for what I believed was best for the country, I always viewed the conflict between the Republicans and Democrats as partisan disagreements. I operated under the assumption that both parties had a shared commitment to the US Constitution and to democracy itself.

I no longer believe that is true.

The GOP has abandoned our democratic ideals. In fact, I am convinced that the current administration is fully committed to destroying our democracy and replacing it with autocracy, in much the same way former President Orbán did in Hungary over the past two decades.

We are months away from the most significant election in our lives—the midterms that will either give the president full reign of power or install a Democratic-dominated Congress that will bring a halt to this illegal and deadly ruling elite. We are at a turning point.

Our country will not be out of danger even if the midterms yield a landslide victory for democracy. The presidential election follows in 2028. It will take every American who believes in self-governance to get involved and stay committed not just to defend our democracy in 2026, but to sustain it into the future.

This is why I wrote this book. I know what it takes to win an election. It takes a sustained commitment, clear goals, and effective strategies and tactics. Everything in these pages comes from direct experience and lessons learned—the tools our Indivisible group and I have tested and refined cycle after cycle. These methods work.

My goal is to help you find the path that fits your skills, talents, resources, and passions. Not everything in this book will be a match for you. But there are many options available that can help ensure that our children grow up in a democracy and do not suffer the oppression of an authoritarian regime.

## How to Use this Book

This is a unique type of book. Here is how to get the most out of what I have to share.

# Part 1
# Unity is Power

I recommend reading each chapter in order, as I share an overview of what we need to accomplish together. In chapters 1-5, my focus is on helping you *get out the vote*. These actions do not require much training, and there are many opportunities for you to find a good fit. You will be connecting with people who support democracy and your goal will be to help them understand how important it is for them to make the effort to vote in the coming elections.

Chapter 6 is for those who want to go a bit deeper into what is called *deep canvassing*—talking with those who hold opposing political views. Usually, this kind of work requires training, but I have included the information because I think it is vital that we all understand the impact of disinformation in our country.

Chapter 7 presents two innovative strategies developed by my colleague Kevin K. Johnson, JD. I included them because in a time of unprecedented challenges we need creative thinking and new approaches.

You may find this material helpful. But know that the strategies and tactics outlined are generally intended to expand the number of Americans who vote in our upcoming elections.

# Part 2
# Strategy by Geographical Area

The information is divided into three stand-alone sections (chapters 8-10), providing you with specific actions you can take depending on where you live or will be campaigning—Blue, Purple, or Red areas. I have organized the material by time frame so you can make the best use of your energy and effort.

## Part 3
## Find Your Team

The third section connects you with organizations that have been vetted for credibility and effectiveness. In Chapter 11, the organizations are grouped in tables by topic or issue. In Chapter 12, you will find all the organizations listed in alphabetical order. I have also included QR codes so you can go directly to their website.

This book has invaluable information for defending our democracy. It's not a long book, but it has powerful tools for you to use.

# PART 1

# UNITY IS OUR POWER

# CHAPTER 1

## The Playbook for the Decade

*Every election is determined by the people who show up.*
**Larry J. Sabato**, PhD
University of Virginia Center for Politics

On April 13, 2026, the Hungarian people voted out a dictator in a historic landslide that shook the global far-right to its foundation. For sixteen years, Viktor Orbán's autocratic regime seemed unstoppable. He methodically undermined Hungarian democracy by capturing the courts, attacking and dismantling the free press, rewriting the constitution to cement his grip on power, while simultaneously building a propaganda machine to silence the opposition. Orbán manufactured enemies by demonizing liberal philanthropist George Soros, the European Union, immigrants, and Ukraine.

Sound familiar?

Donald Trump has been copying Orbán's authoritarian playbook for years.

But now, we can flip the tables and learn from those who removed Orbán from power. Hungary can teach us quite a bit about winning. During those same sixteen years, the resistance organized. They had to be creative and they never gave up.

Orbán may have dismantled public broadcasting and silenced private media outlets—and yet, a stubborn core of independent news outlets survived. They uncovered abuses while shining a light on Orbán's disinformation campaign and corruption that would eventually lead to his undoing in 2026.

Like the inflatable frogs that have mocked Trump at protests in the United States, the satirical "Two-Tailed Dog" party kept younger Hungarians engaged with politics through humor, like promising two sunsets a day and eternal life. They simultaneously exposed the regime's lawlessness, the government's crackdown on civil society, and the assault on democratic checks and balances. All the while, Orbán's corrupt policies, which enriched his allies, began to show cracks as his economy weakened, causing pain for the Hungarian population.

The years of resistance finally delivered in 2024. Orbán loyalist Péter Magyar gave a breakthrough interview to the fledgling independent press that exposed a scandal where the Orbán government pardoned a man convicted of covering up sexual abuse of children. This case struck a raw nerve with the public in a similar way that Marjorie Taylor Greene broke with Trump over the Epstein cover-up. In Magyar's interview, he promised to restore the democratic system of checks and balances, institute term limits, and claw back wealth attained through corruption.

The parallels between Orbán's Hungary and Trump's America are striking. Both have contributed to a weakening economy, a widening wealth gap, and engaged in widespread exploitation which has exposed the vulnerability of both regimes. After the 2024 interview, Orbán tried relentlessly to destroy Magyar, but Magyar and his pro-democracy coalition prevailed by running on a moral imperative to fight corruption and restore integrity, which resulted in a landslide victory.

In the 2026 election, the people of Hungary proved that an entrenched authoritarian machine, no matter how powerful it appears, cannot withstand a tidal wave of dissatisfaction when citizens choose democracy over partisanship. When the people show up and make their voices heard at the ballot box, authoritarianism crumbles.

Now it is our turn.

## America 2026
## Following Hungary's Example

I am writing the final words of this book just a few days after Hungary's stunning change of direction. The timing could not be better for us to savor their success and for Americans to work together for a similar outcome.

> When the people show up and make their voices heard at the ballot box, authoritarianism crumbles.

The information in this handbook is meant for those of you who are distressed about the direction the country has taken and want to do something to reverse course. You may have been involved in activism in the past or this might be your first foray into political action. *Our role in defending democracy for the future of our country cannot be overstated.*

Of course, the hope and the goal is that the United States Government will be restored to the hands of the people by winning back Congress in 2026.

## 2026 November Midterm Elections
## A Necessary Sprint

The November midterm elections are just a few months from now, and we have the chance to replicate the stunning regime change that occurred in Hungary. This book gives you the tools you need to achieve a decisive victory in restoring democracy in America.

It conveys the urgency of the moment and the need to invest time, money, talent, and resources throughout 2026. To be blunt, these are not normal times and everything is on the line. There are no shortcuts: we must give everything we have this year.

The 2026 sprint needs to be front-loaded by raising funds, registering voters, knocking on doors, phone banking, and sending postcards through the summer, then increasing intensity during the final eight weeks before election day, November 3rd.

> **To be blunt, these are not normal times and everything is on the line.**

My goal is to equip as many pro-democracy Americans as possible to get out the vote in 2026; the bulk of this book offers effective strategies that do not require extensive training or experience.

## The Loss in 2024
## Those Who Stayed Home Made an Impact

In 2024, approximately 77,302,580 Americans voted for Donald Trump. In contrast, 75,017,613 votes went to Kamala Harris, and 2,284,977 went to third-party candidates. If third-party voters had supported Harris, the popular vote would have gone to the Democrats. That small number was a deal breaker.

But the more revealing number is the total of Americans who did not vote at all—close to 90,000,000! Engaging with those Americans could have changed the outcome of the election. And that is our goal in the next few months—to re-energize those of us who voted for democracy in 2024 and to expand the number of voters who, for whatever reasons, did not take the time to cast their vote.

This is where you come in. You have the power to make a significant difference in the future of our country. Together, *we have the power* to restore democracy and undo the massive damage caused by the current administration.

My goal is to equip you to engage with those who clearly support democracy and have not fallen for the MAGA deception. The majority of Americans do not want to live in an authoritarian country. So, if they vote, the current administration will be ousted in the same way authoritarianism was overthrown in Hungary.

## Defending Democracy in 2026
## You do not have to be a Democrat
## to Vote Blue

Even though I am a Democrat, I acknowledge that many people are deeply disappointed with the Democratic Party. Some even go so far as saying that the party committed political malpractice during the 2024 presidential election and failed to deliver. They have lost faith and are not motivated to provide it with financial or other support.

But the choice before us right now is not about partisan disagreements. It is time that we lick our wounds and recognize that electoral success is not possible without supporting the Democratic Party on the national and state levels. And it is important to note that the latter is under new leadership and is implementing a plan to overcome past missteps.

The newly revamped Democratic National Committee (DNC), led by Chair Ken Martin and Association of State Democratic Chairs (ASDC) President Jane Kleeb, is focused on learning from past mistakes. The DNC has launched an "organize everywhere, win anywhere" 50-State Strategy that invests in critical infrastructure and staffing, strengthens data and technical operations, and sustains year-round get-out-the-vote operations rather than ramping up only in the months leading up to an election. The strategy reprises a similar approach credited with decisive Democratic victories in the 2006 and 2008 elections.

> If third-party voters had supported Harris, the popular vote would have gone to the Democrats.

The DNC is using the same successful 50-State Strategy that yielded dividends in the 2006 and 2008 elections. The 50-State Strategy was abandoned after President Obama won, which contributed directly to the midterm "shellacking" the Democrats experienced in 2010. The financial stakes are stark. As of the end of 2025, the DNC reported only $14 million in cash on hand and approximately $17 million in outstanding debt, compared to the Republicans' $95 million in cash on hand. We must come together in one unified voice, supporting the DNC, state Democratic parties, and the many highly effective grassroots organizations listed in Chapter 11 on the mission to defeat MAGA. Together, we can amplify efforts to turn out the vote and push back against the worst impacts of the MAGA agenda.

**The Vital Year of 2027**
**Balancing Momentum with Rest**

2027 will be a year of continued resistance against the worst policies of a lame-duck Trump administration. We'll also gear up for an offensive effort to win back the presidency and hold our majorities in the House and Senate. We must not become complacent after the 2026 electoral wins.

History warns us vividly.

In 2004, I canvassed and worked on legal protection in Pennsylvania and was deeply impacted by John Kerry's loss to George W. Bush. I turned my discontent into action and founded the Progressive Action East Bay (PAEB), a grassroots group focused on winning Congress. Our volunteers invested in fundraising and voter turnout for the 2006 midterms, helping take back the House of Representatives. We continued our efforts to help elect Barack Obama in 2008 — and then prematurely declared victory. Feeling our mission was accomplished, our group dissolved.

*We paid a steep price:* the right-wing Tea Party won resoundingly in the 2010 midterms, not only checking Obama's presidential ambitions but winning a majority of state governorships and legislative chambers. This positioned Republicans to draw favorable electoral maps after the 2020 census — maps that to this day provide significant advantages to the Republican Party and MAGA.

I regret that complacency. The lesson: pace yourself for a lifelong marathon, staying involved in every election while resting in the off-cycle years.

### Presidential Election of 2028
### All-Out Sprint

The 2028 presidential election will be consequential, presenting an opportunity to retake the White House while holding onto power in Congress. *Winning is essential*: it will allow us to begin repairing the extraordinary damage wrought by the Trump regime and to hold his Cabinet, leadership, and congressional enablers accountable, as the statute of limitations on many civil-law violations will not have run out.

If we achieve resounding victories, we could potentially reform the Supreme Court and possibly secure statehood for the 700,000 residents of Washington, D.C. and the 3.2 million citizens of Puerto Rico who remain unrepresented in Congress.

## The New Era of 2029
## The Long Road of Restoration

We will do all we can to regain power in 2028, but we must keep up the fight — continuing to raise money, register voters, and stay engaged.

Democrats will face continued headwinds as the electoral map shifts to favor Republicans. As people leave the Northeast and upper Midwest and relocate to Florida, Texas, and other states in the South and Southwest, demographic trends are projected to benefit Republicans.

The work does not end with any single election. As we position our movement for significant impact now, we build the foundation for sustained wins deep into the future. Volunteering and organizing for a cause greater than ourselves must be the work of every generation. It does not end with any single election. But it starts — urgently — with the choices we make in the next seven months.

Show up. Organize. Give everything you have to the sprint of 2026. And then prepare for the marathon that follows.

**We are the power.** Now let's use it.

# CHAPTER 2

## The Crises We Face

*Part of the new authoritarianism is to get people to prefer fiction and inaction to reality and action.*
**Timothy D. Snyder**
American Historian

Even though the last election was a year and a half ago, many of us are still grieving. Our grief is not simply over the loss of an election in 2024, but because of the chaos and distress the country has suffered ever since this administration took office in 2025. With the escalation of one chaotic event and tragedy after another, many Americans are feeling confused, defeated, and powerless. No one has successfully put limits on this president.

These feelings are amplified by Trump acting as though he won a mandate, even though he won less than 50 percent of the popular vote and holds razor-thin margins in Congress.

Democrats need only three additional seats in the House of Representatives and four in the Senate to reclaim power. This will allow Democrats to erect guardrails against the Project 2025 agenda, return Democrats to committee chairmanships with subpoena power, and restore inspectors general who will expose agency wrongdoing. Three seats out of 435. That is the gap we are bridging.

This fight is about more than elections. It is about equality under the law, accountability for those in power, freedom from abuse, access to healthcare, protection of marginalized communities and our environment, and the survival of independent institutions — from our courts to our universities to a free press.

**-1-**
**Impoverishing America**
**Wealth Redistribution**

The Republican majority in Congress has failed to protect the American people from the abuses and overreach of an unfit president and a rogue government. They have shown no concern for what it means to be deeply American. They supported the so-called Big Beautiful Bill — more aptly named the Big Betrayal — which was aimed at enriching millionaires and billionaires at the expense of the middle class, working class, and the poor by giving the largest tax cuts in history to the ultra-wealthy.

*This is the largest transfer of wealth from poor to rich in American history.* The top 10 percent of earners are projected to see their income rise by 2.7 percent by 2034, while the incomes of the lowest earners are projected to decline by 3.1 percent.

The bill slashes Social Security and Medicare, including considerably less federal funding for the states, devastating state treasuries. This will blow a hole in the budgets of all states. For example, California is projected to lose $100 billion, which will gut the healthcare system and lead to the loss of thousands of healthcare jobs. It will additionally deprive California of federal funds for education and food assistance. As Simon Rosenberg of the *Hopium Chronicles* says, "Trump is for the oligarchs. We are for the people."

Medicaid not only supports the very poor, but it also serves working families, children, people with disabilities, and nursing home residents. According to the Center on Budget and Policy Priorities, the Medicaid cuts are expected to result in up to seventeen million people losing coverage over the next ten years.

## -2-
## Project 2025
## Health Protections

Mr. Trump and his enablers in Congress and his Cabinet have also been vigorously implementing the Project 2025 agenda with lightning speed, dismantling in real time the government programs that keep us safe, protect the environment, and provide food assistance. During his confirmation hearing, Secretary of Health and Human Services Robert Kennedy Jr. lied to Congress, agreeing not to interfere with vaccines that keep us safe.

Unelected and unconfirmed major campaign donor Elon Musk advised President Trump to freeze foreign humanitarian aid to the US Agency for International Development (USAID). Immediately, this vital service was decimated — legions of personnel fired, leaving aid recipients around the world without access to life-saving food and healthcare.

For six decades, USAID supported humanitarian programs fighting hunger and disease while advancing democracy in the developing world. In its final full year of operation, USAID reached more than fifty million people with food assistance and helped prevent millions of deaths from preventable diseases. The dismantling of USAID has resulted in the deaths of hundreds of thousands of the world's most vulnerable people.

## -3-
## Immigration
## Lack of Due Process

The National Guard and Immigration and Customs Enforcement have been wreaking havoc on due process and the civil rights of United States citizens and undocumented law-abiding residents alike. US Immigration and Customs Enforcement (ICE) has run roughshod over the constitutional protections of the Fourth and Fifth Amendments, which prohibit unreasonable searches and seizures and guarantee due process of law.

## -4-
## Foreign Policy
## Betrayal of Allies

The administration is abandoning the beleaguered people of Ukraine, serving Putin at the expense of the world order. By threatening to invade Greenland, Mr. Trump seriously threatened the NATO alliance, which has been the most successful military alliance in human history and which has helped prevent another world war since its inception seventy-six years ago. His unpatriotic and reckless actions are advancing the geopolitical interests of Russia and China at the expense of our long-standing allies and the stability of the world.

## -5-
## Free Speech
## Undermining the First Amendment

Our independent institutions have served as guardrails preventing any one branch or individual from accumulating too much power. The administration has threatened the independence of the judiciary. Judges who have ruled against the administration have faced threats and political retaliation.

The free press has struggled for several decades and is now facing regulatory harassment from the Federal Communications Commission and frivolous legal challenges. Our colleges and universities are being defunded and pressured to suppress research and teaching that does not align with the administration's agenda.

The stakes could not be higher. We need to commit to doing all we can — now — so that after this year's midterms, our institutions survive and we are still living in a democracy. "We, the People" truly are the last line of defense.

## -6-
## Deep Pockets
## Advantages of Superior Funding

Notwithstanding the momentum building in our favor, headwinds have been gathering that could undermine our hopes unless we commit fully to the 2026 midterm election and beyond. The Republican Party has a far superior financial war-chest and as of this writing, Trump's super PAC stands at over $304 million.

If we do not dramatically step up our fundraising efforts, we will be outspent in November. Republicans will use their financial advantage to fund advertising attacking Democrats and rehabilitating Trump's standing, replacing reality with propaganda.

Outside Republican groups are already running advertising campaigns designed to change the narrative on the economy, inflation, and immigration for competitive races. It is up to us to counter this by raising money early. Early money supports the hiring of on-the-ground organizers who build the infrastructure necessary to win in November.

**-7-**

## Undermining Fair Election
## Nefarious MAGA Campaign Tactics

We cannot underestimate MAGA's campaigning tactics, their fundraising superiority, disinformation, and efforts by Russia and China to interfere with fair elections. The Trump administration has withdrawn support for cybersecurity defenses, exposing the United States to foreign election interference.

We also face the prospect of voter intimidation leading up to and on Election Day — the possibility of Trump declaring a national emergency, troops on the streets in blue cities, and a postal rule providing for delays in postmark processing that could disenfranchise last-minute mail-in ballots. To ensure victory, we need a massive voter turnout with overwhelming numbers.

Worried about keeping Republican control in the House and Senate, in the summer of 2025, Trump persuaded the Texas Governor to call a special legislative session to approve a new congressional map designed to open up five additional red seats. California voters responded by overwhelmingly approving Proposition 50 — a redistricting plan aimed at shifting five additional congressional seats toward the Democratic column to counteract GOP maps in Texas, Missouri, Ohio, and North Carolina.

With resounding gubernatorial and legislative wins in Virginia in November 2025, Democrats were able to redraw the map and added four new seats in that purple state. Mid-cycle redistricting in Maryland, Wisconsin, and Utah could yield a few additional seats as well. According to Activate America, if everything breaks for Democrats, they could achieve a net gain of two to four congressional seats, while the best Republican case scenario yields up to seven. It will require hard work to secure as many of these seats as possible.

The National Democratic Redistricting Committee is focused on delivering fair electoral maps by pushing back against partisan gerrymandering. For more details go to www.democraticredistricting.com.

Meanwhile, the United States Supreme Court recently emasculated the Voting Rights Act of 1965 which, according to Fair Fight, could jeopardize up to nineteen blue seats. These dynamics underscore the critical importance of joining this fight with a wave-election mindset.

We must be clear-eyed and sober about the battle ahead. To ensure a successful outcome in November, we must not take anything for granted. Complacency is the enemy.

# CHAPTER 3

## We Are the Cavalry

*Courage is not the absence of fear,*
*but the capacity to act despite our fears.*
**John McCain**
Naval officer and former US Senator

Democracy is not a spectator sport. It is a team sport. There are no knights in shining armor — only us, and the hard work we are willing to do together.

Lawyers can defend immigrants in court and push back against government overreach. Artists can design logos, political merchandise, and leaflets. Musicians can raise funds and political awareness.

The good news is that America has come to realize that democracy is worth fighting for. Many Americans want to become more active and do more. It is time to turn grief into resolve — to move from acceptance to action and defend democracy. This must be our life's work.

The most important thing you can do is get involved — today. Not tomorrow or next week. Right now. You do not need to be a seasoned activist to take part in the fight to save our democracy. Whether you are a college student, retiree, or working a day job, you can make a difference. We all have something to offer — whether it is time, a skill, a talent, or financial support.

Look into your heart. What do you have to offer? Each person can contribute in their own way. Regaining power will require sustained and disciplined action to raise money and awareness, register voters, engage in messaging and pressure campaigns, and turn out the vote.

In response to an audience question about what more people can do beyond protesting, MSNOW host Rachel Maddow said: "This is a moment that calls on all of us to do all that we can. The moment calls for all of us to give what we are capable of giving. It does not call on the same thing from all of us. It is never just one thing; there is never a silver bullet. We are a small-d democracy, and the way that democracies heal and advance themselves is by engaging everybody where they are. Whatever work you do, find a way to do it in a way that benefits your country."

## We Have Role Models
## History Shows Us the Way

Countless generations over millennia suffered under autocratic regimes. Constitutional democracies are relatively new when considered against the backdrop of human history.

Many of us who grew up in the United States before the Trump era took our democracy and its freedoms for granted. We are now reminded that every generation is called to step forward to hold the line against attempts to weaken or defeat democracy — whether on the battlefield, with the pen, or by turning out the vote.

In October 2024, while canvassing in Tucson, I recall pulling up to the next house on my list, thinking I would rather be home hiking than knocking on another stranger's door, making my pitch for Kamala Harris for President and Ruben Gallego for Senate.

Then it occurred to me how fortunate I was to have the luxury of doing this — compared to the countless heroes who secured the opportunity for me to exercise my right to be part of our precious democracy.

I thought about how any **Civil War soldier** fighting far from home would have given anything to trade places with me. My short-term inconvenience paled in comparison to the sacrifices they endured. I realized that the least I could do was stop complaining and be grateful for my opportunity to contribute in my small way. After all, I had the added benefit of connecting with kindred spirits who joined me to advance our shared mission.

Over 600,000 Americans lost their lives during the Civil War, many fighting for the principle that all men are created equal, regardless of race or creed. The Reconstruction amendments — the 13th, 14th, and 15th — emerged after that bloody war. It is our turn to defend these hard-won achievements while preserving the democracy so many died to uphold. Thankfully, we are being called this time not with blood, but with our time, talent, resources, and willingness to organize.

Doug Linney, the founder of Activate America, shares the story of his father-in-law, **Lou Vernon — a 21-year-old Quaker medic** who landed at Normandy on D-Day alongside 150,000 others. Lou did not carry a weapon. His job was to run under fire, check on the fallen, dress their wounds, and make life-and-death decisions about who could be rescued. He saved lives and showed courage that day.

Doug told me, "If Lou and his generation — the greatest generation — could face that danger and make the ultimate sacrifice for us, then surely we have an obligation to them, to ourselves, and to future generations to muster the capacity to act despite our fears."

Since we formed our Indivisible group in 2016, I have spent many weekends handing out flyers at farmers markets and transit stops. There are times when I want to sleep in or go home early.

Then I pause and think about how fortunate I am to have the luxury of serving a two-hour shift rather than being tethered to a tour of duty like Lou Vernon, living through a hellscape not knowing if I would survive the day. When it is a choice between enduring on a battlefield for months on end or spending a couple of hours handing out flyers, the choice is easy.

At the signing of the United States Constitution, **Benjamin Franklin** is credited with saying, "We must, indeed, all hang together, or most assuredly we shall all hang separately" — underscoring the importance of unity in the fight for independence. We need that same unity now.

**Congressman John Lewis**, beaten on the Edmund Pettus Bridge on Bloody Sunday in 1965, called it "good trouble" — the necessary disruption of unjust systems through nonviolent action.

He advised: "Do not get lost in a sea of despair. Be hopeful, be optimistic. Our struggle is not the struggle of a day, a week, a month, or a year. It is the struggle of a lifetime. Never, ever be afraid to make some noise and get in good trouble, necessary trouble." This is the spirit that energizes and guides us into 2026.

Our movement calls us to lean in like **Rosa Parks**, who stepped into history and refused to relinquish her seat on the Montgomery bus. This ordinary woman did an extraordinary thing that helped inspire and fuel the civil rights movement.

Environmental activist **Erin Brockovich** followed her conscience when, as a legal clerk, she took on Pacific Gas and Electric on behalf of a small California town suffering elevated cancer rates, ultimately winning a record $333 million settlement.

More recently, **Minnesotans** inspired the nation by mobilizing to protect their neighbors against ICE raids during a bitter winter — teachers, healthcare workers, clergy, small-business owners, and neighbors came together in rapid-response networks that tracked ICE movements and provided food, transportation, and legal assistance to those detained.

Thirty-nine-year-old artist and website developer **Ashley Fairbanks** played a key role in those Minnesota efforts. She started with a simple Google Doc listing resources to support people during the ICE occupation. That document morphed into a mutual aid hub called Stand With Minnesota, which helped raise close to $20 million for rent, transportation, and legal assistance. Her story illustrates that movements are built not from the top down but from the bottom up, by ordinary people who take action.

An example of this type of effort is the **1985 Live Aid** concert, watched by nearly 2 billion people in 150 countries, raised over $127 million for famine relief and demonstrated the power of music to move people at scale.

Bruce Springsteen recently captured it well when he said: "The last check on power, after the checks and balances of government have failed, are the people — you and me. It is in the union of people around a common set of values that is all that stands between democracy and authoritarianism. At the end of the day, all we have got is each other."

Years from now, how will you answer the question of what you did when it really mattered? This is our opportunity to accept the gravity of the moment and become consequential players in this important chapter of history.

# CHAPTER 4

## The Data Proves Our Power

*There is nothing wrong in America that can't be fixed
with what is right in America.*
**Bill Clinton**
42nd President of the United States

Tens of thousands of volunteers who made phone calls, wrote postcards, and walked precincts leading up to the November 2024 election came away demoralized, wondering whether their efforts had mattered. They did. They matter enormously.

Postmortem analysis by Activate America showed that, in the races where they invested, volunteers improved outcomes by 2 to 4 percent in battleground races. Just a 2 percent shift in a congressional district of 300,000 voters yields an additional 6,000 votes — the margin that decided more than two dozen House races in 2024. Without these efforts, there would have been fewer Democratic wins. And because the MAGA margin of power is paper-thin, there is a very small gap to bridge in 2026 to regain power in Congress.

In every election, even in more normal times than these, far too many people stay home. Ninety million people stayed home in the 2024 election. In a country this evenly divided, your involvement can make all the difference — especially when you consider that Trump won

Michigan, Wisconsin, and Pennsylvania by just 230,000 votes combined.

## Support for Democracy
## The Signs Are Encouraging

A number of events have taken place, indicating a significant shift in public opinion. Here is a short list of hopeful indicators.

- The Democratic presidential candidate won the national popular vote in seven of the last nine elections, and Democrats outperformed Republicans broadly in the 2018, 2020, and 2022 elections and in the special elections of 2023 and 2025. The 2025 elections delivered resounding repudiations of MAGA, strongly favoring Democrats and highlighting a notable erosion of support for the Trump regime.
- Democrats won the Wisconsin Supreme Court race in 2025, trouncing the Elon Musk-backed candidate by double digits and maintaining a narrow liberal majority on the court in a crucial swing state.
- Democratic governors in 2025 routed Republican challengers by 15 and 13 points in the Virginia and New Jersey races, respectively, while expanding margins in their state legislatures.
- In 2025, Democratic Socialist Zohran Mamdani won big in the New York mayoral race by a margin of 8.8 points.
- That same year, Democrats won two Georgia Public Service Commission seats for the first

time in nearly 20 years and captured the Miami mayor's office after almost thirty years.

- They broke a Republican Senate supermajority in the Mississippi state legislature and defeated a voter suppression referendum on the Maine ballot by double digits. These victories were a decisive repudiation of the destructive first year of Trump's second term.

- On top of these wins, Democrats have increased their margins with voters, with 37 percent identifying as Democrats and 31 percent as Republicans.

- Democrats hold a six-plus-point margin on the generic congressional ballot — similar to the advantage they held entering the resoundingly successful 2018 midterm, when they flipped forty-one House seats, the largest midterm outcome since the 1974 post-Watergate elections. The Democratic base is notably more motivated to vote than the Republican base, with 66 percent registering intense enthusiasm for the 2026 midterm compared to 50 percent for Republicans.

In addition to these shifts, we see that the president's overall approval is at record lows, with double-digit negative sentiment on his performance on the cost of living, democracy, Medicaid and Medicare, Social Security, corruption, election integrity, jobs, healthcare, and free speech.

Taken together, Democrats have clear advantages in voter affiliation, motivation, and the generic ballot, combined with strong overperformance in the 2025 election cycle and Trump's poor poll numbers. Historical trends favor the party out of power in midterm elections. The wind is at our backs. But wind alone does not win elections. People do.

## Authoritarianism
## The Pressure to Isolate

Because authoritarian movements are designed to isolate people — breaking down unions, civic organizations, and community groups to rob people of their collective identity and power — joining together is itself a form of resistance.

Harvard political scientist Robert Putnam, in his landmark study, *Bowling Alone*, documented the decline of civic engagement in America since the 1970s. It found that people who join civic organizations are also healthier, happier, and more resilient when facing stress. By starting or joining a grassroots group, you are investing in your own well-being while contributing to the political outcome you desire.

Psychologist Martin Seligman, whose groundbreaking research on learned helplessness shone a light on the antidote to powerlessness, invites us to take action — because action reinforces the belief that we can make a difference.

A 2019 study published in the journal *Political Behavior* concluded that political volunteering yields significantly higher levels of life satisfaction than passively consuming the news from the sidelines. People not only feel good about paying it forward — they benefit from the social connection that comes with organized political activity. You build relationships with kindred spirits who share your values and concerns as you work to address your worries.

Consider how much time and energy we expend complaining to friends, coworkers, and family about the state of our democracy. If we calculated the total hours spent in worry and despair on a daily, weekly, or monthly basis, we would be stunned. Were we all to invest a portion of that time helping push change in a positive direction, we could change what we are complaining about. Action is the antidote for anxiety.

# CHAPTER 5

## Your Action Plan

*In any moment of decision, the best thing you can do
is the right thing, the next best thing is the wrong thing,
and the worst thing you can do is nothing.*
**Theodore Roosevelt**
26th President of the United States

After the 2016 election, many of our friends and family were paralyzed by the relentless bad news, unable to navigate dystopian times. We came together and formed an Indivisible group.

The Indivisible movement, founded in December 2016 by Ezra Levin, Leah Greenberg, and other former congressional staffers, launched more than 6,000 groups across the country. Their activist guide generated millions of constituent calls, town hall appearances, and local political events that contributed to the 2018 midterm wave.

Having a common cause restores purpose, builds momentum, lifts spirits, reduces despair, increases effectiveness, and reminds us we are not alone. I call it political therapy — leaning in together as part of a great cause.

If we did it, so can you. To get started, identify co-founders who can bring their own networks of friends and family. Inaugurate your group by advertising a save-the-date on social media or by email and develop an agenda that addresses your mission and suggested activities.

Then register your group at indivisible.org so that volunteers outside your immediate network can find you. Whether you create a new Indivisible group or join one, consider making it real by signing a commitment pledge.

In addition to organizing and strategizing during regular meetings, groups often invite speakers to share relevant books, articles, and organizations with which to collaborate.

Our grassroots Indivisible group has road-tested several initiatives and strategies in recent years that helped move the needle blue. As described in this book, they will help propagate democracy across the country.

**-1-**

## Make Contact
## The Power of Praise and Criticism

Politicians are keenly sensitive to constituent calls, emails, and letters. Contacting local, state, and federal elected officials and state attorneys general really matters. Collective pressure moves the needle and can change opinions. Elected officials track constituents' concerns because they want to be reelected. When enough people speak up on a given issue, it registers a level of urgency that officials cannot ignore.

A 2015 study by communications professors at Michigan State validated the effectiveness of constituent pressure, finding that legislators who received just one constituent phone call were 11 – 12 percent more likely to support the legislation.

Organized, sustained contact campaigns yield results. Consider the recent discharge petition where enough pressure was leveled by constituents in vulnerable Republican districts to change the calculus on how representatives cast their votes regarding the Epstein files.

Download the 5 Calls app, which makes it easy to share your concerns with members of Congress in just a few minutes. The 5 Calls staff research and write scripts that promote progressive positions and provide relevant phone numbers for elected officials. Alternatively, call the United States Capitol switchboard at (202) 224-3121, articulate your position, and tell your story as a constituent.

Town halls hosted by your elected representatives are another powerful opportunity to weigh in. Politicians may change their position if they perceive a groundswell of support or opposition on an issue.

If your representative refuses to hold a town hall, consider organizing an Empty Chair town hall to highlight their fear of facing constituents. The 2017 Empty Chair campaign, organized by Indivisible groups in competitive districts, contributed directly to the failure to repeal the Affordable Care Act. That tactic works.

### -2-
### Write Letters to America
### The Resolutions Project

The *Hopium Chronicles* is leading an effort to highlight to members of Congress the unprecedented attack on our federal government and constitutional order. The project replicates how our Founders built support for the Revolution — by having towns across the colonies introduce, debate, and pass resolutions condemning the Crown, which raised awareness of the Crown's "injuries and abuses" and created local ownership of the fight for independence.

In the years preceding the *Declaration of Independence*, local assemblies, town meetings, and committees of correspondence linked activists across the colonies. The Resolutions Project is a twenty-first-century version of this tactic.

The Resolutions Project encourages democratically controlled legislatures, city councils, and county boards of supervisors to approve condemnations of the Trump administration, with freedom to highlight whatever concern rises to the top in their community. Consider approaching your state legislature, city council, or board of supervisors and invite them to approve a resolution of condemnation.

**-3-**

**Raise Funds
Early and Often**

If we underestimate Trump's ability to rehabilitate his standing by the midterms, we do so at our own peril. After the 2022 midterms, Trump's approval rating was as dismal as it is today.

Yet by spending big and early, he dramatically improved his poll position and made the 2024 election competitive. We must not allow that to happen in the lead-up to 2026.

Front-loading fundraising allows candidates to hire staff and set the narrative early in the election cycle.

Our Indivisible group pioneered a strategy of hosting remote virtual fundraisers — Parties for Democracy — in the lead-up to the 2020 presidential election.

Our campaign raised $450,000 in just three months during the summer of 2020, supporting vetted grassroots organizations including the Lincoln Project, Activate America, HeadCount, Fair Fight, Democracy Forward, Commit to Democracy, Vote Forward, among others. In our experience, virtual Parties for Democracy require only 4 to 5 hours to plan, yield higher turnout than in-person events, considering the investment of time, and raise an average of $9,000 per party in a single hour via videoconference. They can reach friends and family across the country regardless of whether you live in a red, purple, or blue region. For a step-by-step toolkit, consult indivisible-raeb.org/parties-for-democracy.

The virtual Party for Democracy model has been proven at scale and is replicable by virtually anyone with a computer and a network of friends. We have found that people are more likely to give when asked by someone they know. Our hosts have raised between $8,000 and $10,000 per party during a one-hour video call. Imagine if every one of the nearly 2,500 active Indivisible groups hosted a single virtual Party for Democracy — the total raised would approach $25 million.

You can also support grassroots organizations directly. For example, you can consider contributing to Hopium's Audacious Expansion Fund, which aims to make Florida and Texas more competitive while focusing on flipping the Senate in Alaska, Iowa, Maine, Ohio, and North Carolina.

Or organize your own in-person fundraising event or concert. A house party, benefit concert, or community event can raise both money and awareness in your local network.

**-4-**
**Reach Out to Your Community**
**Economic Pressure**

Set up at your local farmer's market, transit stop, or shopping center, and connect patrons to opportunities to plug in by donating money or time to effective grassroots organizations in battleground districts and regions.

Our local Indivisible group partners with Activate America, Commit to Democracy, Flip the Vote, and other organizations focused on vulnerable Republicans in swing districts. Our volunteers enjoy connecting with neighbors and are regularly thanked for the guidance they provide.

We develop flyers offering commuters and shoppers opportunities to get involved — alerting them to upcoming marches, protests, boycotts, and grassroots organizations where their donations will make the biggest difference.

As circumstances change, we refresh our messages and become trusted messengers to those we encounter. In 2025, we began handing out Know Your Rights flyers in English and Spanish, then shifted to supporting the Wisconsin Supreme Court race, then targeted seventeen vulnerable Republicans seeking reelection, then promoted California's Proposition 50, and then pivoted to our Buying Blue for the Holidays campaign, discussed below.

The farmers market table is not only a vehicle to connect with patrons — by showing up week after week, you become a trusted source of civic guidance. It is an effective means of connecting with your community and recruiting volunteers to the mission.

On the economic front, consider a buycott — actively supporting companies that share your values and financially support Democrats. The Goods Unite Us app, created in response to the Supreme Court's Citizens United ruling, lists thousands of companies and scores them based on their political donations using Federal Election

Commission data. With millions of consumers flexing their economic muscle by voting with their dollars, we can exert economic and political pressure on corporations that fund our opponents.

After the November 2024 election, our volunteers — donning festive blue Santa caps — distributed leaflets at farmers markets promoting our Buying Blue for the Holidays campaign. Our flyers included a QR code directing patrons to the Goods Unite Us app.

Patrons were thrilled to learn, for example, that Peet's Coffee donates 63 percent of its political contributions to Republicans while Starbucks gives 89 percent to Democrats. Consider launching a Buy Blue campaign as a way to inform your community and channel consumer power toward democratic values.

**-5-**
**Get-Out-the-Vote**
**Proven Methods**

At the end of the day, the goal of a campaign is to win, and to do that we must increase turnout among supporters. This effort is known as Get-Out-the-Vote, or GOTV. During voter outreach, it is vitally important to encourage early voting. The following methods are listed in rough order of personal impact per contact.

Knocking on doors is the most effective way to contact voters — face-to-face, going door-to-door. While it is the most labor-intensive tactic, each conversation is more likely to translate into a vote. Many campaigns pair first-time volunteers with experienced canvassers or encourage volunteers to bring a friend and canvass in pairs.

The ground game is not primarily about persuasion — it is about helping targeted voters who already support our candidates to show up at the polls. The landmark research by Donald Green and Alan Gerber established that face-to-face canvassing increases turnout by approximately seven percentage points per contact — far more than any other method.

Phone banking is the next most effective GOTV tactic. Calling allows real conversations without the travel time of door-to-door canvassing, so a campaign can reach more voters with fewer volunteers. Phone calls produce roughly 3 to 4 percentage points of lift per contact when they result in a live conversation, and about one percentage point when they leave a voicemail.

Handwriting postcards is an easy, personal way to reach voters that has grown significantly in recent election cycles. Postcarding has become an entry point for new volunteers not yet ready to knock on doors or make phone calls, and a social anchor for volunteer groups who host postcard-writing parties. Handwritten postcards generate roughly 1-2 percentage points of additional turnout per contact, with greater impact when received close to Election Day.

Text banking can be incredibly effective for sharing time-sensitive election information — registration deadlines, links to find polling places, early voting start dates, and other vital logistics. Text messages produce approximately 0.5-1 percentage point lift per contact. Targeted, informational texts from a real person still cut through.

These numbers may seem small in isolation, but their cumulative effect across a large-scale, with a well-organized ground operation can be decisive in close races.

Early voting is critically important as it allows campaigns to identify and remove supporters from the active contact list as they vote. This enables organizers to concentrate resources on targeted voters who have not yet voted. It reduces the risk that illness, family emergencies, transportation problems, or deliberate voter suppression on Election Day will prevent a supporter from voting. Every supporter who votes early is one fewer person the campaign needs to mobilize on November 3rd, when every volunteer and every minute of campaign infrastructure is stretched to its limit.

**-6-**
**Register Voters**
**The Focus with Impact**

Registering people to vote is essential to expand the electorate — it is particularly important where we want to flip red seats blue. Given that control of the White House and Congress has been decided by tens of thousands of votes in recent cycles, finding and turning out new voters can be the deciding factor in 2026, 2028, and beyond.

The registration gap is urgent. Between 2020 and 2024, Republicans registered 2.4 million new voters while Democrats lost 2.1 million registered voters in the thirty states that track party registration. Front-loading registration efforts during the spring and summer of 2026 is essential. Here are the most effective ways to register voters in your community:

- Contact your state Democratic Party and join their registration drives.

- Work with a local League of Women Voters chapter.
- Join a national effort through vote.org or download the vote1234.com voter app.
- Visit your local community college or university and register students on campus.
- Set up at your local farmer's market in its free speech zone.
- Volunteer with HeadCount or Rock the Vote and register voters at concerts.

College campuses deserve special strategic attention. Students are legally entitled to register at their campus address in most states. We must counter the Republican registration advantage with systematic, sustained, community-by-community voter registration efforts.

-7-
## Protest
## And What Comes Next

Since Trump entered the Oval Office, people have risen in record-breaking numbers to protest his authoritarian grab for power. The third No Kings Day protest during March 2026 may have been the largest single-day protest in American history, with over eight million people turning out in all fifty states.

To put that number in context: the Women's March of January 21, 2017 — the largest single-day protest in American history prior to the No Kings protests — drew an estimated four million people. The March for Our Lives in 2018 drew approximately two million. The George Floyd protests in the summer of 2020 involved between 15 and 26 million people over several weeks. The energy is there. The question is whether we can organize and harness it.

During the first No Kings protest, our team posted ten volunteers who handed out 1,500 flyers connecting protesters to specific opportunities — pressuring vulnerable Republicans facing reelection to stand up to Donald Trump by writing postcards, making phone calls, and financially supporting the grassroots organizations leading the effort. That day, we also recruited forty new volunteers to our Indivisible group.

The next day, as I was offering one of these flyers to a woman at a farmers market, she responded: "I did my part and marched yesterday at No Kings." She was emblematic of the vast majority of protesters who posted their pictures on social media and felt they had done their part. Yet protesting is only one form of activism.

Mass protests are critically important at this perilous moment in history, but protests by themselves — especially one-off protests — rarely produce lasting results. Nonetheless, marches and protests serve as an ideal opportunity to recruit volunteers to the cause.

Although protests are just a part of the solution, joining a protest for a day and calling it good will not solve the problems we are protesting against. Many are eager to do more.

As Indivisible co-founder Ezra Levin said after the first No Kings protest: "Even though it was one of the largest protests in history, it is still a protest. It is a tactic, and a tactic is not enough to achieve your goals. A tactic is part of a broader strategy: mass, persistent, peaceful protest. The real question is, how successfully do we channel the millions of newly engaged Americans into productive, on-the-ground organizing?" A successful movement channels outrage into strategy.

**-8-**

### Protect Voter and Election Integrity
### Be Prepared

Whether we enjoy another year of free and fair elections will depend, in part, on attorneys challenging Trump's attempts to undermine them. The Trump administration has attempted to seize voting machines, requested voter lists from states, and deployed dry-run efforts to intimidate voters — particularly voters of color. Trump illegally deployed the National Guard to Los Angeles and Chicago and sent ICE to Minneapolis and other cities.

Lawyers and paralegals willing to step forward can stand in the way of efforts to suppress the vote in blue and purple congressional and Senate races. Several organizations train and coordinate legal volunteers to protect elections, including the Lawyers' Committee for Civil Rights Under Law, Common Cause, and Fair Fight. *If you are an attorney or paralegal, consider signing up for voter protection training in the months prior to Election Day.*

At the national level, the Lawyers' Committee for Civil Rights Under Law has deployed thousands of volunteer attorneys to manage voter roll challenges, Election Day incidents, and post-election litigation. State Democratic parties lead election protection programs that coordinate poll observers, hotline volunteers, and legal response teams. Locally, attorneys can join a county Democratic Party and serve as precinct observers or legal advisers.

**-9-**

## Know Your Rights
## Constitutional Observers and
## Immigration Protection

The Trump administration has greatly expanded pressure on immigrants, moving well past long-standing enforcement to practices that clearly exceed constitutional and legal limits. Immigration issues have become important not just to protect immigrants, but as a broader focus for organizing against the administration's excesses.

The Fourth Amendment protects all persons from unreasonable searches and seizures, and the Fifth

Amendment guarantees due process, regardless of citizenship status. ICE agents have violated these constitutional protections by illegally detaining people without a judicial warrant, entering homes without consent, and arresting American citizens based on their appearance. Constitutional observers play a critical role in documenting violations, deterring bad behavior, and providing evidence to support legal challenges.

National and local groups — including the Immigration Legal Resource Center, the ACLU, and other grassroots organizations — provide trainings covering individual constitutional protections against arbitrary detention and arrest.

Many groups also distribute multilingual red cards summarizing key rights: the right not to speak with agents or sign documentation; the right to deny access to homes and private areas without a judicial warrant; and the fact that ICE administrative warrants do not constitute probable cause to search a vehicle, home, school, or business.

Rapid-response networks aim to prepare communities to identify when ICE enforcement actions may be underway, convey that information to local networks and hotlines, and encourage volunteers to rapidly deploy to active locations. Minnesota teachers, nurses, clergy, small-business owners, and neighbors inspired the nation by standing up peacefully for their targeted neighbors in frigid temperatures — observing and documenting ICE actions to protect rights and hold the federal government accountable. The DNC is now collaborating with the Immigrant Defense Network to train tens of thousands of constitutional observers to safely monitor, document, and report on ICE actions as non-confrontational witnesses.

**-10-**
**For the Future**
**Run for Office or Recruit Someone Who Should**

The future of our movement also rests on the shoulders of those willing to run for office. Consider running for — or inviting others to run for — a local school board, utility board, or city council seat. Volunteering on a planning commission or other local board serves the community directly and can lead to later runs for elected office. Building the bench of future Democratic leaders is a long-term investment in the health of our democracy.

*As you can see, there is a wide variety of opportunities for you to be part of the solution. Focus on which tactics line up with your skills, talents, and interests.*

# CHAPTER 6

# Disinformation and Deep Canvassing

*Those who stand for nothing fall for everything.*
**Alexander Hamilton**
American statesman and Founding Father

This chapter focuses on deep canvassing, which is different from the traditional canvassing activities previously discussed. Deep canvassing is a long-term voter-engagement strategy designed to shift public opinion. It involves active listening to understand a voter's life experiences and values while sharing personal stories to build a genuine rapport to change hearts and minds on divisive issues

If you choose to engage in these more challenging conversations, you will find some helpful information here.

We need to realize that there are people who do not simply disagree with each other; we are actually living inside a different version of reality than the one you know. Not just different opinions. Different facts.

They have been told false things, over and over, by sources they trust. They have been told that the mainstream media lies, that elections are stolen, and that Democrats want to destroy the country they love. And they have heard all of this so many times, from so many directions at once, that it feels completely real to them.

This is not an accident. It is the result of a decades-long, well-funded effort to build a bubble — a media world designed to keep conservative voters angry, afraid, and cut off from outside information. Understanding how that bubble works is the first step to breaking through it.

The challenge for campaigners is not simply that voters have been misled. It is that the people doing the misleading have a plan, serious money, and a massive platform — and for most of the last thirty years, the response has been to fight back with facts. Facts alone do not work.

A voter who has been told for years that the mainstream media is the enemy of the people will not change their mind because a canvasser quotes *The New York Times*. Something different is required. This chapter is about what that looks like.

## STEP 1
## Know How Disinformation Works

Before you can push back against disinformation effectively, you need to understand why it works so well. The answer is not that people who believe false things are foolish. The answer is that disinformation is carefully designed to take advantage of the way all human minds work — including yours.

### -1-
### We All Filter the News
### Through What We Already Believe

People do not read or watch the news with a blank slate. We take in new information through the lens of what we already think is true. Stories that fit our existing beliefs feel right and stick easily. Stories that challenge our beliefs feel suspicious, and we often reject them without really thinking about why. Researchers call this confirmation bias. It is not a flaw found only in conservatives, Trump supporters, or people without college degrees. Every human brain does it. Those who create disinformation know this and design their content to slide right into whatever their audience already believes.

**-2-**
## It is Built to Make You Feel, Not Think

Disinformation is not mainly an argument. It is an emotional experience. Content designed to make people feel afraid, angry, or outraged spreads faster, lands harder, and gets shared more than content designed to simply inform. Social media platforms make this worse because they are built to grab attention, and nothing grabs attention like something that makes you feel threatened or furious.

When people are flooded with strong emotion, clear thinking takes a back seat. That is not just a figure of speech — it is how the brain actually works. The part of the brain that weighs evidence and thinks things through gets pushed aside by the part that is reacting to danger. The people behind disinformation understand this. You need to understand it too.

## -3-
## Attacking the Message
## Feels Like Attacking the Person

For many people who watch Fox News or follow MAGA media, those sources are not just where they get their news — they are where they feel at home. Their media world is wrapped up in their sense of who they are, who their people are, and what they stand for. When you challenge what they heard on Fox, it does not feel like a fact-check. It feels like an attack on them personally. That is why walking up to someone and saying "that's not true" almost always makes things worse, not better. The most effective campaigners know how to lead with something in common rather than leading with a correction.

## -4-

## Hearing Something Over and Over
## Makes It Feel True

Repetition alone can make a false claim feel real. Studies have shown that the more often people hear something — even something they initially doubted — the more believable it becomes. The right-wing media machine runs on this principle.

The same talking points get repeated across right-wing news channels, websites, and social media, all at the same time, hitting people from every direction at once. No amount of fact-checking can keep up with that kind of saturation. That is why trying to correct false information after the fact rarely works on its own.

The bottom line for campaigners: you cannot argue someone out of their identity, and you cannot talk someone out of an emotion with a list of facts. Knowing why disinformation works is not just interesting background — it is the foundation of being effective at your job.

## STEP 2
## Know Your Own Blind Spots

This part is important, and it goes for all of us. The tendency to believe things that confirm what we already think does not skip over Democrats, progressives, or people who read serious newspapers. It is a human thing, not a political thing.

Deep canvassers who show up to conversations acting like they have all the answers, who get visibly frustrated when someone believes something different, who treat voters like problems to be fixed rather than people to be heard — those campaigners are less effective, not more.

Take a look at your own news diet. Are you reading from a real variety of trustworthy sources, or mostly from things that tell you what you already agree with? Are you familiar with the strongest version of the arguments you disagree with, or just the easy-to-dismiss versions? The deep canvasser who says, "I have looked at this carefully from different angles, and here is what I actually found," is far more credible than one who sounds like they are reading from a script.

People will not hear you out until they feel like you have heard them. That is not a trick or a technique — it is just how conversation works. Trust gets built through real attention, not by going through the motions. When a voter tells you something you know is not true, do not jump straight to the correction. Get curious first. What does this person actually care about underneath this? What are they worried about? Where might there be common ground?

You also do not have to have all the answers. "I do not know the answer to that, but I will find out and get back to you," goes further than a confident response you cannot actually back up. People are used to being told what they want to hear by politicians and campaign workers. Admitting what you do not know is one of the most disarming things you can do.

## STEP 3
## Know Who You Are Talking To

Not everyone caught up in disinformation got there the same way. Good deep canvassers learn to quickly read the person in front of them, because different situations call for different responses.

### -1-
### The Casual News Scroller

This voter gets most of what they know from Facebook or scrolling through their phone. They have not spent much time thinking about where their news comes from, and they probably do not realize that what shows up in their feed has been selected by an algorithm designed to keep them clicking — not to keep them informed.

Casual news scrollers are not deeply committed to any particular media identity. They are just seeing what the platform puts in front of them. This voter is often the most reachable. A friendly suggestion — framed not as "you have been lied to" but as "here is somewhere that gives you the full story" — can go a long way.

The Associated Press, Reuters, PBS NewsHour, and NPR are trusted by a wide range of people across the political spectrum and are good places to point someone.

### -2-
### The Fox True Believer

This voter's sense of self is tied up in their media world. Fox News is not just a channel to them — it is their community and their team. If you go straight at what they heard on Fox, you will almost certainly get their guard up rather than their mind open.

The better move is to find something you genuinely have in common first. Nearly everyone, regardless of politics, worries about being able to pay the bills, keeping their family safe, and leaving something decent for their kids. Start there. Build some real rapport. You are not going to change a Fox loyalist's mind in one conversation. What you can do is leave a door open.

### -3-
### The Person Who Does Not Know What to Believe

This voter is overwhelmed. The news is coming from everywhere, it often contradicts itself, and they have given up trying to sort it out. They may believe several conflicting things at once or just check out entirely. But they are reachable — not through political arguments, but through simple, practical guidance.

Give them a short list of specific sources and a plain reason to trust each one: "The AP has been covering news without a political agenda since 1846. Reuters reports from around the world and has no reason to take sides in American politics. PBS and NPR are publicly supported and consistently rated among the most accurate news outlets around." Giving people a concrete starting point makes a real difference.

**-4-**
**The True Believer**

This voter is not confused. They know what they believe, and they are actively pushing it on others — whether because they are fully convinced or because they enjoy the fight. You are very unlikely to move them during a doorstep conversation, and trying for too long may just give them more energy. Be polite, keep it short, and move on. Not every conversation is worth the time.

**STEP 4**
**Know What Actually Works**

If correcting false information after the fact does not work, what does? The best answer the research has found is to get ahead of the lie before it lands.

Think of it like a vaccine. A vaccine works by giving your immune system a small, safe preview of a threat so it knows how to fight back when the real thing shows up. The same idea applies to disinformation.

When you warn someone in advance that a certain manipulation trick is coming — without necessarily naming the specific lie — they are much better prepared to recognize and resist it when it arrives. Studies back this up: people who have been warned about a manipulation tactic are significantly less likely to fall for it later.

For deep canvassers, this means getting out in front rather than playing defense. Instead of waiting for a voter to repeat a false claim and then trying to undo it, you name the trick before it reaches them.

**-1-**

**Deal With a False Claim
With The Truth Sandwich**

When you do have to address a false claim directly, try the truth sandwich: start with what is true, briefly mention that a false version is out there, then come back to what is true. Never open with the lie. Every time you repeat a false claim — even to argue against it — you plant it a little deeper in the listener's memory.

The structure is simple: true thing first, quick mention of the false version, true thing again. The truth gets said twice, and it is the first and last thing they hear.

**-2-**

**Ask Questions
Instead of Correcting**

People are far more likely to rethink something when they work through it themselves than when someone tells them they are wrong. This is a well-established finding from counseling and conflict resolution, and it works just as well when canvassing on a doorstep.

Instead of saying "that is not true," try "where did you hear that?" or "what would change your mind about this?" or "what matters most to you when it comes to this issue?"

These questions invite thinking instead of shutting it down. They are also much harder to just walk away from.

**-3-**
**Slow Down**
**The Power of the Pause**

One of the simplest things that actually reduces the spread of false information is getting people to slow down before they hit share. Research shows that simply asking someone to think for a moment about whether something is accurate before passing it on makes a real difference — not because they suddenly become expert investigators, but because the question breaks the automatic reflex that drives most sharing.

When you are talking with voters, you can encourage this habit: "Before you share something, it is worth asking — do I actually trust where this came from, or does it just feel true because it got me worked up?"

**Conclusion**
**Disinformation Is a Democracy Problem**

Disinformation is not primarily a media or technology problem. It is an attack on democracy itself. The efforts to suppress votes, flood the zone with lies, stoke outrage through algorithms, strip cities of local news, and hand media outlets to politically connected billionaires — these are not separate issues.

They are pieces of the same strategy, all aimed at convincing people that their vote is pointless, the system is rigged, nothing will ever change, and no one in power can be trusted.

When people hear that message long enough, they stop trying. Researchers call this learned helplessness — the state you reach when you have been told so many times that your actions do not matter that you stop taking action. The low voter turnout and political disengagement we see in so many communities is not laziness or apathy. It is the predictable outcome of a sustained campaign designed to produce exactly that result.

The answer to learned helplessness is not a better ad or a smarter algorithm. It is one person showing up for another person. A neighbor at the door. An actual conversation. The experience of being taken seriously by someone who looked you in the eye and meant it. That is something no media machine can replicate. That is what you are doing.

Thomas Jefferson wrote in 1787 that he would rather have newspapers without a government than a government without newspapers. He understood that people cannot govern themselves without good information, and good information requires a press that is free and honest.

Both of those things are under serious attack right now. The answer is not to give up or to retreat into media that only tells us what we want to hear. It is to go out and have the harder conversations with the people who are hardest to reach, knowing what we are up against and knowing what actually works.

Making the case for a different direction cannot be made with facts alone. It takes genuine understanding, real credibility, and honest respect for the person on the other side of the door — especially when what they believe makes that hard. Not everyone chooses to have these conversations. In case you do, this information will be of some guidance.

# CHAPTER 7

# Two Strategies for Pro-democracy Action

*The problem is whether the American people have loyalty enough, honor enough, patriotism enough, to live up to their own Constitution.*
**Frederick Douglass**
American Author and Abolitionist

I am including two ideas developed by my colleague, Kevin K. Johnson, MA, JD, that I believe have great merit and potential. Both are fundamental elements of his new book, *The American Oath Project: Protecting the Backbone of Democracy.*

## -1-

## The American Oath Project
## A New Legal Path to Presidential Accountability

Most people have been hanging their hopes on removing Trump via impeachment and conviction or by the Cabinet invoking the 25th Amendment. The former would require sixty-seven Senators to convict while the latter would require the Vice President and a majority of the Cabinet to find that the president is "unable to serve" due to incapacity. Neither scenario is plausible because it is highly unlikely that 20 Republicans would join the 47 Democrat

Senators to convict. Nor can we expect a supine Cabinet to declare the president unfit to serve. But there is another way, and it does not run through Congress or the Cabinet.

Kevin Johnson lays out a litigation strategy grounded in contract law rather than constitutional politics. The US Constitution is defined as a contract of employment between the United States and the President.

When Trump took the oath of office, he swore to "preserve, protect and defend" the Constitution and to "faithfully execute" the laws of the United States. However, Trump willfully and intentionally lied when he made those promises.

Under long-standing contract common law (known as "fraud in the inducement") the contract was void at its inception because a trove of evidence indicates that Trump never intended to honor the Constitution when he took the oath. A court could rule that the contract never legally existed and render every executive order Trump issued during his second term legally void.

## Breach of Contract

Trump's conduct, and that of much of his administration, includes many hundreds of material breaches of the agreement he made with the American people. Some of the documented violations include: unauthorized military actions; directly and indirectly threatening federal judges and defying federal court orders; denial of due process regardless of documented status; politicization of the military and the elimination of military legal counsel; the assault, battery, and even killing of citizens protesting ICE operations; illegal deployment of National Guard troops; the conversion of ICE into a masked, badge-free paramilitary force conducting warrantless searches and arrests; and threatening and harassing the press, universities and individuals around the country who have disagreed with Trumps policies and programs. The list goes on and on.

A court finding that these transgressions represent material and cumulative breaches of contract could find that the presidential employment contract is rescinded — meaning Trump would simply be out of a job.

## Who Can Bring These Suits?

These cases can be brought by states, nonprofit organizations, citizen groups, or individuals directly harmed by a wide range of Trump's unconstitutional actions. Members of Congress, for example, who have publicly called on the military to resist illegal orders — Senator Mark Kelly and Senator Elissa Slotkin among them — would have standing to sue. So would the Epstein victims, whose constitutional rights to seek redress of their grievances have been repeatedly subverted by efforts to hide documents and other evidence of wrongdoing.

A Supreme Court majority (5 – 4) that has already ruled against Trump on tariffs and troop deployments (and is poised to rule against him on birthright citizenship) would eventually be asked to rule on whether the oath to uphold the Constitution means something or nothing. More pointedly: the choice would be between democracy and dictatorship.

## What You Can Do Now

Mr. Johnson calls on all citizens to express gratitude to and support for all those in the country who have taken oaths to uphold the Constitution. This includes veterans (over 18 million), National Guard troops, active-duty military, federal judges, civil servants, and law enforcement.

He also urges everyone to write to their governor and state attorneys general, urging them to pursue civil lawsuits on these contract/constitutional grounds.

Further, everyone should contact nonprofit organizations that are capable of, or are currently litigating against, the administration to originate or add claims targeting Trump's continued tenure. The urgency of bringing these civil actions is underscored by Trump's plans to interfere in the midterm elections.

The courts could also be asked to restrain Trump's plans to interfere with free and fair elections. Trump could be enjoined from attempts to suppress the vote based on the legal theory of "anticipatory breach of contract." Contract common law provides that you do not have to wait to be damaged when it is clear that the other party to the contract will breach it.

All these approaches involve, for the first time, truly going on the offense against Mr. Trump and not just reacting to his next move.

For more information, please visit The American Oath Project.com

## -2-
## The Oath Peace Symbol

Our movement needs a symbol for which to rally around that aligns with our values and serves as a visible, everyday expression of our shared commitment to the Constitution, to each other, and to peaceful political action.

The Oath Peace Symbol is especially important to serve as a counterweight to Trump's bellicose behavior, communicating what we stand for, not just what we oppose. He regularly attacks people and organizations who disagree with him; has been undermining our democratic institutions; and literally waging and/or threatening war around the globe.

### Two Foundational Documents

The Oath Peace Symbol is rooted in the founding ideals of the United States. Its design draws on two core sources:

- **The Declaration of Independence**
  *"We hold these truths to be self-evident, that all men are created equal, that they are endowed by their Creator with certain unalienable Rights, that among these are Life, Liberty, and the pursuit of Happiness."*

- **The Preamble to the Constitution**
  *"We the People of the United States, in order to form a more perfect Union, establish justice, ensure domestic tranquility, provide for the common defense, promote the general welfare, and secure the blessings of liberty to ourselves and our posterity..."*

## Powerful American Symbols

The images and words within the symbol were chosen deliberately:

- **The American Flag** — red for valor and bravery, white for purity and innocence, blue for vigilance, perseverance, and justice — anchors the design. Its thirteen stripes and stars represent the original colonies and honor those who have worked to fulfill the American promise.
- **The Bald Eagle** represents freedom, independence, and strength. The Dove is the long-standing symbol of peace and new beginnings.
- **The Statue of Liberty** calls to mind the country we have tried to be — one that has welcomed and benefited from immigrants across generations — and reminds us to treat all people with respect and fairness. The raised right hand has traditionally represented honesty and commitment. Here it also represents the act of taking an oath to uphold the Constitution.

The words *Life, Liberty, and Happiness* reflect the promise at the heart of the American story. *Oath* recognizes all who have sworn to defend the Constitution. *We the People* speaks to the principle that government derives its authority from citizens. The word *Democracy* is supported by *Equality* and *Truth*, and everything within the outer circle is surrounded and embraced by the values found in both the Constitution, the amendments that make up the *Bill of Rights* and the *Declaration of Independence*.

## Why It Matters Strategically

The symbol is meant to be worn and displayed — on hats, pins, shirts, jewelry, armbands, water bottles, signs, vehicles, backpacks, and stationery. You do not need to wait for the next march or rally to show where you stand.

At public gatherings and protests, the Oath Peace Symbol can serve as a conspicuous sign of peaceful intent to anyone present with guns (e.g., law enforcement, National Guard troops, and active-duty military).

Additionally, the symbol would make a clear statement to any court that might later consider whether demonstrators were in fact intending to be peaceful. The symbol reinforces a commitment to free speech and assembly and should help deter any heavy-handed government response. Staying peaceful is essential as widespread violence will be seen by the administration as grounds to declare martial law and invoke the Insurrection Act.

## The Invitation

Wearing the Oath Peace Symbol every day is an important way to signal your belief in democracy, the rule of law, and the rights of all people. It is a reminder — to yourself

and to those around you — of what we are working
toward.

For more information, visit:
theamericanoathproject.com

# PART 2

# STRATEGY BY GEOGRAPHICAL AREA

# CHAPTER 8

## What to Do If You Are in a Blue District

*True patriotism springs from a belief in the dignity of the individual, freedom and equality not only for Americans but for all people on earth.*
**Eleanor Roosevelt**
Activist and former First Lady of the United States

Living in a blue district is not a reason to sit on the sidelines — it is a strategic asset that needs to be deployed. The elections that will determine the balance of Congress in 2027 will be decided not in San Francisco or Manhattan or Chicago, but in the competitive swing districts across the country where margins are measured in thousands of votes.

Your most powerful contribution is to direct your money, your time, and your energy outward — toward those battlegrounds where what you do will matter most. Volunteers, donors, and organizers in blue districts and fuel and support the ground game in purple regions of the country.

Your farmers market table raises money to support the ground game in the battleground states while phone banking will reach voters in tight races across the country

**SPRING 2026**
**Build Your Foundation**

## -1-
## Join or Form a Grassroots Organization

The most important thing you can do right now — before the fall campaign season, before the ground game kicks into full gear — is to find your organizational home. An Indivisible group, Activate America, Commit to Democracy, or any of the more than eighty organizations listed in this book, will give you a structure, a community, and a set of tasks that are already coordinated with the broader electoral strategy.

Acting alone is less effective, more exhausting, and more likely to burn you out before November. Acting within an organization means your energy is multiplied by everyone around you and directed toward the activities with the highest documented impact.

If there is no group in your community, consider forming one. An initial meeting of your friends, neighbors, colleagues, and family members who are willing to commit to a regular schedule will get you started. You can seek guidance from the tools the national Indivisible[1] organization offers on its website.

---

[1] https://indivisible.org/resource/guide/

# -2-
# Raise Funds

The financial gap between the Democratic Party and the Republican apparatus is stark: As of late 2025, the Republican Party had $95 million while the DNC had only $12 million.

That gap cannot be closed by large donors alone — it will be closed by tens of thousands of people hosting small and mid-size fundraising events and directing their proceeds to the grassroots organizations and state Democratic parties working in competitive districts.

Virtual Parties for Democracy (PFDs)[2] are among the most cost-effective fundraising tools available to individual activists. They require only four to five hours of planning, can be organized around any occasion — a birthday, an anniversary, a themed gathering — and, on average, generate eight thousand to ten thousand dollars per event through a one-hour video call.

Unlike in-person events, they reach friends and family across the country regardless of where they live, turning your personal network into a national fundraising operation. Our Indivisible group raised $450,000 in three months during the summer of 2020 using this model. Imagine the impact if even a fraction of the 2,500 Indivisible groups across the country adopted it.

Additional fundraising pathways include direct support for grassroots organizations listed in this book. For example, contributions to the *Hopium Chronicles*[3] Audacious

---

[2] https://www.indivisible-raeb.org/parties-for-democracy
[3] https://www.hopiumchronicles.com/p/hopiums-audacious-expansion-fund

Expansion Fund, will target competitive Senate and House races. Other options include in-person events, such as house parties or benefit concerts, that raise both funds and volunteer energy within your local network.

### -3-
### Register Voters

Between 2020 and 2024, Republicans registered 2.4 million new voters while Democrats lost 2.1 million registered voters in the thirty states that track party registration. That registration gap is one of the most important and under-discussed vulnerabilities going into 2026. Closing it requires front-loaded effort in the spring and summer — before fall campaign season, before registration deadlines, and before civic energy has a chance to dissipate.

College campuses are among the highest-yield voter registration environments: young voters are both highly registerable and increasingly motivated by the current political climate, and a single afternoon on a campus quad can produce dozens of new registrations. Farmers markets, transit stops, and community events in your blue community are also productive, particularly for reaching people who are sympathetic but have not yet formalized their registration.

Contact your state Democratic Party to identify where registration drives are most needed and how to plug into the existing infrastructure. Organizations including Head-Count, Rock the Vote, and Vote.org provide training, materials, and coordination support.

**-4-**

## Make Your Voice Heard

Using the 5 Calls app to contact your representatives takes only a few minutes and is most effective when done consistently rather than occasionally. Your representatives in a safe blue district need to hear from constituents who want them to fight vigorously against the Project 2025 agenda — to use every procedural and oversight tool available to slow the administration's most damaging actions.

Representatives track constituent contact volume because it signals the intensity of feeling in their district, and sustained contact pressure on a specific issue can shift a legislator's public posture even when their vote seems safe. Thank those who are fighting hard and make clear to the ones who are not that their comfort is not guaranteed.

Town halls and community meetings are also valuable for building the visible constituency that representatives need to justify aggressive action. Even in a safely blue district, organized, visible, engaged voters shape how your representatives present themselves and what risks they are willing to take.

**-5-**

## Reach Your Community

Serving as a trusted messenger at your local farmers-market, supermarket, or transit stop is one of the highest-leverage activities available to blue district residents. You are not trying to persuade people who disagree with you — you are connecting people who already share your concerns but do not know what to do about them to specific, actionable opportunities.

In our experience, the vast majority of people who stop at an activist table are grateful for the guidance and genuinely relieved to find something concrete they can do. Many of them will become volunteers themselves.

Your role at these community touchpoints is to direct money and volunteer time outward: to the purple districts where canvassing will happen, to the grassroots organizations coordinating the ground game, to the voter registration drives in communities where new voters will make the difference. Every flyer handed out, every QR code scanned, every conversation that ends with someone taking a next step is part of the operation.

**-6-**

## Protest and March

Protests and marches create moments of collective energy that are genuinely valuable for sustaining motivation over a long campaign. The most valuable thing you can do at a march is use it as a recruitment and redirection opportunity: bring flyers that show people how to move from protest to action, recruit volunteers for phone banking and canvassing operations, and make the case that showing up at a march and then going home is not enough. The people who leave a protest and immediately join a grassroots organization are the ones who change the outcome. Be the person who makes that connection.

**-7-**

## Get Training as a Constitutional Observer

Communities that have been supported by their neighbors in moments of vulnerability are communities that show up. Your presence as a constitutional observer is not just legal protection — it is a statement about what kind of community you are building. The DNC's collaboration with the Immigrant Defense Network provides training for constitutional observers across the country.

Constitutional observers — trained volunteers who legally document and monitor law enforcement actions — have proven to be one of the most effective tools for protecting vulnerable communities from illegal government overreach.

In Minnesota, trained observers standing silently at ICE operations and documenting what they saw on video had a measurable deterrent effect on aggressive enforcement behavior and provided the evidentiary basis for subsequent legal challenges. This is not confrontation — it is witness, which has a long and honorable history as a form of civic protection.

Training is available through the DNC's collaboration with the Immigrant Defense Network, the Immigration Legal Resource Center, the ACLU, and local grassroots organizations. The skill of knowing your rights — and helping others know theirs — is one of the most durable contributions you can make to your community regardless of what happens in November.

★ ★ ★ ★ ★

## SUMMER-FALL 2026
### Turn Out the Vote

The fall ground game is where elections are won or lost, and your role as a blue district resident is primarily to export your capacity to the places where it is most needed.

### -1-
### Knock on Doors

Knocking on doors is the single most effective GOTV tactic available. Face-to-face conversation produces the highest conversion rate from contact to vote, and it is the activity that campaigns can never fully staff with professional employees.

The goal is mobilization, not persuasion — helping voters who already support Democratic candidates to actually show up at the polls. Pair with a friend for safety and motivation. Many of the most committed long-term activists report that their best friendships were formed with people they canvassed with.

## -2-
## Phone Bank

Phone banking allows you to reach more voters with less travel time. Fewer people answer their phones than a decade ago, but the conversations that do happen — particularly with voters who are on the fence about whether to bother — are highly effective.

Modern phone banking platforms are user-friendly, provide scripts and voter data, and allow you to volunteer from your own home. Even an hour a week in the months before November adds up to meaningful contact volume.

## -3-
## Text Bank

Text banking is particularly effective for time-sensitive logistic information — registration deadlines, early voting dates, polling locations, ballot tracking links. Voters who receive a personalized text from a real person rather than an automated system are significantly more likely to engage and follow through on voting. Text banking is also highly accessible for volunteers who are newer to political action and not yet ready for phone calls or door-knocking.

## -4-
## Write and Mail Postcards

Postcard writing has emerged as one of the most social and accessible volunteer activities of the last several cycles. Handwritten postcards to targeted voters in competitive districts carry a personal weight that no digital outreach can replicate. Organize postcard-writing parties

— bring people together, make it a social occasion — and leave with new volunteers who are now invested in the outcome.

★ ★ ★ ★ ★

# THE DAY OF THE ELECTION

Consider taking Election Day off from work entirely. The final push — door-knocking, ride provision, poll watching, voter reminder calls — is the highest-impact use of a volunteer's time in the entire cycle, and the campaigns in competitive districts are always understaffed for it.

If you can travel, even for a weekend, to a purple district within driving distance, the impact of your presence is substantially greater than remote phone banking. Our volunteers have found competitive congressional races in the California Central Valley within easy driving distance from the Bay Area. Others have spent weekends in Reno or Las Vegas. Traveling with friends makes it an experience worth repeating.

## Voter and Election Protection

Protecting the integrity of the 2026 midterm elections will require an army of trained legal volunteers. There will be vigorous attempts — by foreign actors, by domestic operatives, and potentially by the administration itself — to challenge results, intimidate voters, and create procedural obstacles to certification in competitive districts.

If you are an attorney or paralegal, voter protection training through the Lawyers' Committee for Civil Rights

Under Law, Common Cause, or Fair Fight is one of the highest-leverage activities you can undertake before November. If you are not a legal professional, you can support election protection efforts as a trained poll observer, a voter assistance volunteer, or a ride-to-the-polls coordinator. Every role in this infrastructure matters.

## POST-ELECTION
### Fall 2026 and Beyond

### Buy Blue for the Holidays

After the election, pivot your community outreach from voter turnout to economic pressure. The "Buy Blue for the Holidays" campaign invites shoppers to vote with their wallets by supporting companies whose political giving aligns with Democratic values.

The Goods Unite Us app uses Federal Election Commission data to score thousands of companies based on their political contributions, making it easy to produce shareable flyers with specific, local recommendations. In our experience, people are genuinely surprised and motivated by specific information — learning that one coffee chain donates heavily to Republicans while a competitor gives heavily to Democrats is exactly the kind of concrete, actionable data that changes behavior. Order blue Santa hats to draw attention to your table and make the campaign visually memorable.

## Recruit Candidates for Office

The Democratic bench — the pipeline of credible candidates for state and federal office — is built at the local level, one school board seat and city council race at a time. The people who run for local office gain the name recognition, fundraising experience, political relationships, and governing track record that make them competitive for higher office.

Without that pipeline, the party is perpetually dependent on celebrity candidates who lack deep community roots. Identifying people in your community who have the qualities of effective leadership — and actively recruiting them to run, offering to volunteer on their campaigns, and supporting their early fundraising — is one of the most durable investments you can make in the long-term health of democratic governance.

## Put Your Commitment in Writing

Now that you have reviewed the many ways you can put your commitment to democracy into action, I recommend that you actually write down your goals and intentions. At the end of Part 2, there is a pledge form you can fill out and sign.

We all have good intentions, but life often gets in the way. Putting your commitment in writing helps you follow through—and sharing it with friends and family creates accountability. Feel free to share with others.

# CHAPTER 9

# What to Do If You Are in a Purple District

*The vote is precious. It is almost sacred. It is the most powerful nonviolent tool we have in a democracy.*
**John Lewis**
US Congressman and civil rights activist

If you live in a swing congressional district or a competitive Senate state, you are at the center of the map. The outcome of the 2026 midterms will be decided not by the most reliably blue or red parts of the country but by the places where the margins are close, the voters are genuinely persuadable, and the ground game makes the difference between winning and losing.

That means you — not metaphorically, but literally. Your presence on the ground in your own community, your conversations with your neighbors, and your visibility as someone who is organized, engaged, and willing to talk about why this election matters are more valuable than all the money and remote phone banking in the world. Campaigns spend millions of dollars trying to replicate the effect of a trusted neighbor showing up at a door. You can do that for free. The question is whether you are willing to.

Recent special elections and polling suggest that many districts previously written off as safely red may be far more competitive than anyone assumed a year ago.

The political environment strongly favors Democrats; the generic ballot advantage is substantial; and voter enthusiasm among Democratic-leaning constituencies is running well ahead of that among Republicans. None of that translates automatically into votes. It translates into votes when it is organized, mobilized, and when the people who should be winning are actually doing the work.

★ ★ ★ ★ ★

## SPRING 2026
## Build Your Foundation

### -1-
### Join or Form a Grassroots Organization

In a purple district, joining a grassroots organization is not just a good idea — it is essential. The difference between an uncoordinated collection of motivated individuals and an organized group working from the same voter data, the same messaging, and the same strategic calendar is the difference between activity and impact.

Organizations like Indivisible, Activate America, and the state Democratic Party have spent years building the infrastructure — the lists, the training, the coordination with campaigns — that allows volunteers to focus on the activities that actually move votes rather than reinventing the wheel.

If you are already in a group, deepen your commitment. Identify two or three people in your network who are not yet organized and bring them in. If you are not yet in a group, finding one should be your first action after finishing this chapter.

This book lists more than eighty organizations operating across the country. Your state Democratic Party can connect you with the local chapter most active in your district.

Think realistically about the time you currently spend on political anxiety — reading alarming news, discussing the situation with friends, worrying about outcomes you feel unable to influence. Now imagine redirecting even a quarter of that time into organized action in your own district. The transformation in your sense of agency alone would be worth it. The transformation in the electoral outcome would be more so.

## -2-
## Raise Funds

Fundraising in a purple district serves double duty: it directly funds the campaigns and organizations working in your district, and it builds the community of committed donors who will sustain the effort through the full campaign cycle. The financial disadvantage facing Democrats in 2026 is real and significant, and it cannot be overcome without broad-based small and mid-size donor activity across competitive districts.

Virtual Parties for Democracy" (PFD)[4] are the most accessible and cost-effective fundraising format available to individual activists. They require only four to five hours of planning, can be structured around any occasion, and generate an average of eight to ten thousand dollars through a single one-hour video call by leveraging your personal network.

_____________________

[4] https://www.indivisible-raeb.org/parties-for-democracy

Critically, they reach your network across geographic lines — friends and family in blue districts who cannot canvass in your district can write a check, and a virtual party gives them a concrete, social occasion to do so. The funds raised can be directed to local campaigns, state party operations, or the grassroots organizations listed in this book that are most active in your district.

**-3-**

## Register Voters

In a purple district, voter registration is not a background activity — it is a frontline strategic priority. Every unregistered voter who leans Democratic in your district is a potential vote that the opposition cannot respond to. The registration gap that opened between 2020 and 2024 is a structural vulnerability that can only be addressed by sustained, proactive registration work beginning now, not in October.

Community colleges and universities are the highest-yield registration environments: students are legally registerable at their campus address, are disproportionately motivated by the current political climate, and are systematically underrepresented on voter rolls. A regular presence at your campus student union or quad — just a few hours on a weekend — can produce dozens of new registrations per visit.

The key is consistent presence over time rather than one-off drives. Voters need to see that there is an organized community effort behind the registration push. Contact your state Democratic Party to understand where registration gaps are largest in your district and how your efforts can be coordinated with the broader statewide strategy.

# -4-
# Make Your Voice Heard

As a resident of a swing district or a competitive state, your calls to elected representatives carry more weight than calls from safely blue or red districts. Your representative or senator knows that you are a voter who could go either way — that your support is not guaranteed and your opposition is not meaningless. Use that weight consistently.

The 5 Calls app makes it easy to identify the right representatives and provides talking points on current issues. Sustained contact pressure on a specific issue registers as a political signal that representatives take seriously, particularly on issues like healthcare, Social Security, and the cost of living, where public opinion in even purple districts runs counter to the administration's policies.

Town halls are where constituent pressure becomes most visible and most uncomfortable for representatives who are not delivering. Organize or attend meetings hosted by your congressional representative — particularly if they are a vulnerable Republican.

For representatives who refuse to hold town halls, organizing an Empty Chair event — a public meeting in their district with a literal empty chair where they should be sitting — is a powerful way to draw media attention to their avoidance and signal to persuadable voters that their representative does not trust them enough to show up. Consult the national Indivisible[5] organization for detailed guidance on organizing these events effectively.

---

[5] https://indivisible.org/resource/guide/

-5-

## Reach Your Community

As a resident of a purple district, your community out-reach has an immediacy and credibility that outside volunteers cannot replicate. You are not a stranger from a blue city showing up to tell people what to think — you are a neighbor who lives here, whose family shops at the same stores and knows the same people. That credibility is enormously valuable in communities where outside political intervention is viewed with suspicion, and it is something that only you can provide.

Set up at your local farmers market, transit stop, or community event, not to lecture but to connect — to share information about how people can get involved, to answer questions, and to direct people who are already motivated toward specific opportunities to act. In our experience, the vast majority of people who stop at an activist table are not opponents looking for an argument — they are curious neighbors who want to do something and do not know how. Be the person who shows them the way.

-6-

## Protest and March

Protests in a purple community have a particular strategic value beyond the demonstration itself: they make visible the size of the organized opposition in a district that politicians and media often assume is more conservative than it actually is.

A well-attended march in a swing district signals — to the incumbent, to the media, to persuadable voters who wonder whether they are alone in their concerns — that the community is not monolithic and that dissent is organized and significant. Attend protests not just to express yourself but to recruit: bring flyers that direct protesters toward the specific, sustained actions that produce votes, and use the energy of the event to add names to your volunteer list.

**-7-**

## Get Training as a Constitutional Observer

In a purple district, the communities most vulnerable to aggressive immigration enforcement are often the same communities whose voter turnout will determine the margin of victory.

Constitutional observer training — learning how to legally document, monitor, and report on law enforcement actions without confrontation — is one of the most direct ways you can protect your neighbors while also building the trust and relationships that translate into civic engagement over time.

★ ★ ★ ★ ★

**SUMMER-FALL 2026**
**Turn Out the Vote**

This is the season for which everything else has been preparation, and in a purple district the ground game is not a supplement to the campaign — it is the campaign. The voter data, the canvassing lists, the phone banking scripts, and the GOTV coordination are all in place.

What they need is bodies: volunteers willing to spend their weekends walking precincts, their evenings making calls, and their lunch hours writing postcards.

## -1-
## Knock on Doors

Door-to-door canvassing is the highest-return activity in the entire electoral toolbox. A face-to-face conversation at a voter's door is five to ten times more likely to produce a vote than a mailer or digital ad.

In a district decided by a few thousand votes, the difference between a fully staffed and understaffed canvassing operation can be the difference between winning and losing.

Canvass in pairs — it is safer, more motivating, and produces better conversations. Treat each shift as a commitment to your community, not an optional activity you do when you feel like it.

## -2-
## Phone Bank

Phone banking produces real conversations with voters who are on the fence about whether to bother voting — the most movable segment of the electorate. Modern phone banking platforms are easy to use, provide all the information you need, and allow you to volunteer from home.

A consistent two-hour session per week in September and October adds up to meaningful contact volume, and the conversations that happen in the last weeks before an election are among the most persuasive interactions that any campaign produces.

## -3-
## Text Bank

Text banking delivers time-sensitive logistic information — early voting dates, polling locations, ballot tracking, registration deadlines — to voters who may not answer their phones but will read a text. In the final weeks before an election, texts from real people rather than automated systems have a significantly higher engagement rate and are particularly effective for younger voters who communicate primarily through messaging.

## -4-
## Write and Mail Postcards

Postcard writing is accessible, social, and surprisingly effective. Handwritten postcards to targeted voters in your district carry a personal weight that no digital outreach can replicate. Organize postcard-writing parties that are also volunteer recruitment events — bring people together, make it a social occasion, and leave with new volunteers who are now invested in the outcome.

★ ★ ★ ★ ★

## THE DAY OF THE ELECTION

Please take Election Day off from work if you possibly can. The final push on Election Day — last-minute door-knocking, voter reminder calls, ride provision for voters who need transportation, poll observation — is chronically understaffed in every competitive district, and the volunteers who show up on Election Day produce a disproportionate share of the final margin.

**Voter and Election Protection**

In a purple district, election protection is not a peripheral concern — it is a core strategic priority. Attempts to challenge results, intimidate voters, and create procedural obstacles to certification are most likely to occur in the very close races that will determine the House and Senate majorities.

If you are an attorney or a paralegal, signing up for voter protection training through the Lawyers' Committee for Civil Rights Under Law, Common Cause, or Fair Fight should be one of your first priorities this summer. If you are not a legal professional, you can serve as a trained poll observer, a voter assistance volunteer, or a ballot tracking coordinator.

Every role in the election protection infrastructure is essential, and in a district that could be decided by a few thousand votes, a robust protection operation can be the difference between a win that holds and a win that gets litigated away.

★ ★ ★ ★ ★

## POST-ELECTION
## Fall 2026 and Beyond

### Buy Blue for the Holidays

After the election, shift your community presence from voter turnout to economic pressure. The "Buy Blue for the Holidays" campaign connects people to the Goods Unite Us app, which uses Federal Elections Commission data to score companies based on their political giving.

In a purple community this campaign has particular resonance: it gives people who are not deeply political a concrete, daily action that expresses their values without requiring them to become activists. Consumer behavior, aggregated across a community over time, sends a real economic signal to businesses that political alignment has consequences.

### Recruit Candidates for Office

In a purple district, the quality and credibility of Democratic candidates for local, state, and federal office is a significant determinant of electoral outcomes. Down-ballot races for school board, city council, state legislature, and county government matter both for the policies they produce and for the bench they build.

A strong local Democratic candidate in a close district can drive turnout among voters who might otherwise stay home, introduce the party to communities that have been underserved by Democratic organizing, and build the grassroots relationships that make future campaigns easier.

If you know someone who has the qualities of effective leadership — a neighbor, a colleague, a community leader — actively encourage them to consider running, offer to volunteer on their campaign, and connect them with the state party.

## Put Your Commitment in Writing

We all have good intentions, but life often gets in the way. Putting your commitment in writing helps you follow through—and sharing it with friends and family creates accountability. Consider signing the pledge at the end of Part 2 and copying it to share with others.

# CHAPTER 10

# What to Do If You Are in a Red District

*Our political leaders will know our priorities only if we tell them, again and again, and if those priorities begin to show up in the polls.*
**Peggy Noonan**
American Journalist

If you live in a red congressional district or a deeply red state, you may have spent the last several years feeling politically invisible — surrounded by neighbors whose views seem incompatible with your own, with no competitive race nearby to organize around, and with little sense that anything you do locally will affect the national outcome. That feeling is understandable, but it is not accurate.

Recent special elections and sustained polling have revealed that the political map is considerably more fluid than it appeared even a year ago. Districts that would have been written off as unwinnable in 2023 have become genuinely competitive.

The Trump administration's deep unpopularity across a wide range of specific issues — healthcare, Social Security, cost of living, corruption — has eroded support in communities that voted for him by large margins just a year or two ago.

The Democratic National Committee's fifty-state strategy, launched under new leadership in 2025, is specifically designed to invest in organizing infrastructure in red states and districts rather than conceding them as permanently lost. You have more agency than you realize. What follows is a practical guide for using it.

★ ★ ★ ★ ★

## SPRING 2026
## Build Your Foundation

### -1-

### Join or Form a Grassroots Organization

In a red district, the first and most important thing you can do is find your people. The isolation of being a Democratic activist in a heavily Republican area is real, and it is one of the primary reasons that progressive organizing in red communities tends to be sporadic and burn-out-prone rather than sustained and effective.

Joining or forming an Indivisible group or another grassroots organization does not just give you something to do — it gives you a community, a network of people who share your concerns and your commitment, and the organizational structure that allows individual effort to add up to collective impact.

These groups also serve a crucial intelligence function: they are embedded in local communities in ways that national organizations are not, and they understand the specific concerns, values, and pressure points of their neighbors far better than any out-of-state campaign can.

That local knowledge is an asset that no amount of national organizing can replicate, and it is one that you are uniquely positioned to develop and deploy.

Think about how much time you currently spend feeling frustrated and isolated. Now think about what it would mean to spend even a fraction of that time in the company of like-minded neighbors, working toward a shared goal. The community you build in the process of organizing is itself one of the most valuable outcomes of political engagement.

**-2-**
**Raise Funds**

In a red district, fundraising for competitive races elsewhere may feel counterintuitive — but it is one of the highest-impact activities available to you. Your personal network almost certainly includes people in blue and purple districts who are looking for effective ways to contribute to the broader effort.

A Party for Democracy (PFD).[6] gives your entire network — regardless of where they live — a social occasion and a concrete mechanism for directing money to the organizations and campaigns that will determine the congressional majority.

Virtual parties require only four to five hours of planning and generate an average of eight to ten thousand dollars per event. You do not need to live in a competitive district to host one. You need a network of people who care about the outcome and a willingness to organize an event that gives them the opportunity to act.

---

[6] https://www.indivisible-raeb.org/parties-for-democracy

The funds you raise can be directed to the Hopium Chronicles Audacious Expansion Fund[7], which is specifically focused on regaining power in Congress.

Secondly, the fund supports efforts to rebuild Congress in states like Florida and Texas to be more competitive over time — building the long-term infrastructure that will eventually make your own community less red.

## -3-
## Register Voters

The DNC's fifty-state strategy is premised on the insight that there are Democratic-leaning and genuinely persuadable voters in every community in America — and that they have historically been underserved by a party that concentrated its organizing resources in places it was already competitive.

Registering voters in a red district is a long-term investment in the changing demographics and political composition of your community, and it is a contribution that compounds over time as those registered voters develop a habit of civic participation.

College and community college campuses are the most target-rich registration environments in any community. Young voters are disproportionately Democratic-leaning and disproportionately unregistered, and a consistent campus registration presence — even in a red area — can produce meaningful numbers of new voters over the course of a registration season.

---

[7] https://www.hopiumchronicles.com/p/hopiums-audacious-expansion-fund

Farmers markets and community events that draw diverse audiences are also productive. Contact your state Democratic Party to learn how your registration efforts can contribute to the broader statewide voter file, ensuring that the voters you register are tracked, contacted, and turned out in November.

## -4-
## Make Your Voice Heard

Constituent pressure works even in red districts — sometimes especially in red districts, where Republican representatives assume their constituents are uniformly supportive and are caught off guard by organized, persistent opposition.

The discharge petition that produced Republican votes for the release of the Epstein files is one example. The town hall pressure campaigns that forced Republican members to publicly defend their positions on Medicaid and Social Security are another. Constituent contact volume is tracked by every congressional office, and a sustained increase in calls on a specific issue registers as a political signal that representatives take seriously regardless of their party.

Use the 5 Calls app to make regular, focused calls on the issues where Republican support is most vulnerable — cost of living, Social Security, Medicare, and healthcare — areas where public opinion, even in red districts, runs against the administration's actual policies. For representatives who refuse to hold town halls, organizing an Empty Chair event draws media attention and signals to persuadable voters that their representative is avoiding accountability rather than earning it.

## -5-
## Reach Your Community

Farmers markets and community events in red areas tend to draw audiences that are more politically diverse than the surrounding community's voting patterns might suggest.

Many people in red communities are deeply dissatisfied with the current direction of the country but have no organized community around them to make that dissatisfaction feel legitimate or actionable. Serving as a trusted messenger in these spaces — not as a partisan advocate but as an informed neighbor who can explain what is at stake and how people can make a difference — can reach voters who would never attend a Democratic Party meeting or respond to a campaign mailer.

Your message at these outreach points should be primarily directional: here is where the competitive races are, here is how you can help from wherever you live, and here is what an hour or a week of your time could actually contribute to the outcome.

People who feel politically powerless in their own communities often respond strongly to the realization that they can have a meaningful impact on a race elsewhere — that geography is not destiny when it comes to electoral organizing.

## -6-
## Protest and March

Protests in red communities are acts of visibility and courage as much as they are strategic interventions. They signal to other dissidents in the community that they are not alone — that the apparent political homogeneity of their surroundings is not as complete as it seems.

They put local media on notice that there is organized opposition to the prevailing political alignment. And they give people who are politically isolated a community and a sense of shared purpose that sustains engagement over time.

Join and publicize these events, use them to recruit volunteers, and bring materials that direct protesters toward the specific, sustained actions — phone banking, postcarding, canvassing in nearby swing districts — that translate energy into votes.

## -8-
## Get Training as a Constitutional Observer

Red communities are often the sites of the most aggressive immigration enforcement activity, and the people subject to that enforcement are among the most vulnerable in your community.

Constitutional observer training — learning to legally document and monitor enforcement actions without confrontation — is a concrete way to protect your neighbors and build the cross-community relationships that are the foundation of long-term organizing.

The deterrent effect of trained observers has been documented in communities across the country: law enforcement agents who know they are being legally documented on video behave differently than those who believe their actions will go unrecorded. Training is available through the ACLU, the Immigration Legal Resource Center, and the DNC's collaboration with the Immigrant Defense Network

In a red district, you may know people in the military, law enforcement, the civil service, or the judiciary who took an oath to defend the Constitution and who are now being asked — explicitly or implicitly — to follow directives that conflict with that oath.

This is not a hypothetical concern: the Trump administration has repeatedly tested the limits of what officials will comply with, and the compliance of those officials has been one of the primary mechanisms through which democratic norms have been eroded.

If you have friends or family members in these positions, the conversation about what their oath actually requires is one of the most important conversations you can have.

This is not posed as a political argument, but as a question about institutional integrity. What does it mean to serve the country rather than a person?

Military veterans and former federal employees who have already navigated this question can be powerful voices for this message, and connecting people who are wrestling with it to others who have been through it is a concrete and valuable contribution to the health of democratic institutions.

# SUMMER-FALL 2026
# Turn Out the Vote

## -1-
## Travel to Swing Districts

Traveling to a nearby swing district or state for a weekend of door-to-door canvassing is the highest-impact thing you can do from a red area. Many red-leaning areas are within a few hours of competitive congressional districts or Senate battlegrounds. Taking a long weekend in October — particularly the weekend before Election Day — to canvass in a swing district combines maximum personal impact with a genuinely energizing experience. Bring a friend. Make it a tradition.

## -2-
## Phone Banking

Phone banking from your home in a red district can reach voters in competitive districts across the country. Modern phone banking platforms allow you to call targeted voters anywhere in the country, as long as you have an internet connection and a phone.

Even an hour or two a week in September and October contributes meaningfully to the contact volume that produces the final margin in close races.

**-3-**
## Text Banking

Text banking is particularly accessible for volunteers who are newer to political action and want to contribute without the higher-stakes interaction of a phone call. Sending personalized texts to voters in swing districts about early voting dates, polling locations, and registration deadlines is a low-barrier, high-impact activity that anyone with a smartphone can do from anywhere in the country.

**-4-**
## Write and Mail Postcards

Postcard writing to targeted voters in competitive districts is one of the most social and accessible volunteer activities available. Organize a postcard-writing party with your local activist group — combine it with a potluck or any social occasion — and produce hundreds of handwritten postcards that will land on kitchen tables in swing districts in the weeks before the election.

★ ★ ★ ★ ★

## POST-ELECTION
### Fall 2026 and Beyond

### Buy Blue for the Holidays

After the election, the "Buy Blue for the Holidays" campaign using the Goods Unite Us app is an accessible, everyday activism that keeps your network engaged and sends an economic signal to the business community in your area. In a red community, the campaign also has a consciousness-raising function: many people who have not thought carefully about the political implications of their consumer choices are genuinely interested in the information once they have access to it.

The combination of a visible table, a shareable app, and blue Santa hats creates a recurring community presence that keeps your network active and visible in the post-election period when volunteer energy tends to dissipate.

## Recruit Candidates for Office

Candidate recruitment and development in red communities is a long-term investment with compounding returns. The school board members, city council members, and county supervisors who develop their political skills in red districts today are the state legislators and congressional candidates of the future.

Democratic candidates who run credible local campaigns in red areas — even when they lose — shift the political narrative, register new voters, build organizational infrastructure, and keep the party visible in communities that have otherwise been written off.

If you know someone who has the qualities of a strong candidate, encourage them to run. Support their campaign. Help them build the network and the skills they will need for the races ahead. The future of the Democratic Party in red America is being built right now, by people like you who refuse to concede that their community is permanently lost.

## Put Your Commitment in Writing

We all have good intentions, but life often gets in the way. Putting your commitment in writing helps you follow through—and sharing it with friends and family creates accountability. Consider signing the pledge at the end of Part 2 and copying it to share with others.

# MY COMMITMENT PLEDGE

☐ **Join a Group:** I will join or form an Indivisible group or join a grassroots organization.

☐ **Donate:** I will donate to one of the grassroots organizations in this book, the DNC, and/or the state Democratic Party.

☐ **Raise Money:**

    ☐ For my next birthday: no presents—just donations for my virtual Party for Democracy.

    ☐ I will host a house party to raise money and recruit fellow volunteers.

☐ **Register Voters:** I will help register voters and text or invite 20 friends to do the same.

☐ **Retail Connections:** I will hand out leaflets at my local farmer's market.

☐ **Turn Out the Vote:** I will help get out the vote by knocking on doors, making phone calls, and writing postcards in the months leading up to the election.

☐ **Host a Phone Bank:** I will organize a phone banking session for my network.

☐ **Host a Postcard Party:** I will organize a postcard-writing gathering.

☐ **Take Election Day Off:** I will knock on doors and/or make targeted phone calls.

☐ **Voter Protection:** I will engage in voter protection at the polls.

☐ **Visit a Swing State:** I will canvass in a swing district within my state or in a swing state on weekends prior to the election.

☐ **Recruit a Friend:** I will invite a friend to join me in any or all of the above.

☐ **Call My Representatives:** I will make regular calls using the 5 Calls app.

☐ **Attend a Town Hall:** I will show up and make my voice heard.

☐ **Constitutional Observer:** I will complete training to protect my community.

☐ **Buy Blue:** I will support and spread the word about blue companies using the Goods Unite Us app.

**I commit to strategic efforts to
win the Presidency and retake the Senate
and the House of Representatives**

Hours/Month__________

Money: $__________

Signature: ______________________________________

*Note: Consider copying this Commitment Pledge
and sharing it with friends and family to create
accountability.*

# PART 3

# FIND YOUR TEAM

# CHAPTER 11

## Organizations by Topic

| Campaign Finance Reform | |
| --- | --- |
| **Organization** | **Description** |
| **Equal Citizens** equalcitizens.us/ | Works to fix democracy by establishing truly equal citizenship |
| **Issue One** issueone.org/ | Builds bipartisan power to strengthen the foundations of American democracy |
| **Center for American Progress** americanprogress.org/ | Progressive policy think tank |

| Changing System | |
| --- | --- |
| **Organization** | **Description** |
| **Braver Angels**<br>braverangels.org/ | Brings Americans together across political divides to reduce polarization |
| **FairVote**<br>(Ranked Choice Voting)<br>fairvote.org/our-erforms/ranked-choice-voting/ | Advances ranked-choice voting to create fairer, more representative elections |
| **Goods Unite Us**<br>goodsuniteus.com/ | Reveals corporate political donations so consumers can make informed choices |
| **Green is the New Black**<br>greenisthenewblack.com/ | Provides information on companies that meet stringent criteria around governance, environment, & welfare |
| **Living Room Conversations**<br>livingroomconversations.org | Facilitates respectful, structured dialogue across political & social differences |
| **National Popular Vote**<br>nationalpopularvote.com/ | Works to ensure the presidency reflects the national popular vote |
| **Open Secrets**<br>opensecrets.org | Tracks money in politics to Expose influence and corruption |

| Election Integrity | |
|---|---|
| **Organization** | **Description** |
| **Citizens for Responsibility & Ethics Washington (CREW)**<br>citizensforethics.org | Fights for democracy by building a government that is accountable, transparent & ethical |
| **Common Cause**<br>commoncause.org | Nonpartisan organization fighting corruption & strengthening democratic accountability |
| **RepresentUS**<br>represent.us | Nonpartisan organization working to make government accountable to the people |
| **Public Citizen**<br>citizen.org | Advocates for consumer protections, corporate accountability, & democratic reforms |

| Impactful Donations for Democracy | |
|---|---|
| **Organization** | **Description** |
| **Focus for Democracy**<br>focus4democracy.org/ | Applies rigorous, metrics-based research to recommend where donations have the highest impact |

| Legal Defense of Voting | |
|---|---|
| **Organization** | **Description** |
| **ACLU**<br>aclu.org | Defends civil liberties & constitutional rights through litigation & advocacy |
| **Brennan Center for Justice**<br>Brennancenter.org | Researches, defends, & advances democracy, voting rights, & constitutional governance |
| **Campaign Legal Center**<br>campaignlegal.org | Works on behalf of the American people to hold government accountable |
| **Democracy Docket**<br>Democracydocket.com | Covers voting rights, election litigation, & threats to democratic participation |
| **Democracy Forward**<br>Democracyforward.org | Uses the courts to defend democratic institutions & progressive policies |
| **Free Speech for People**<br>freespeechforpeople.org | Defending the constitution & working toward political equality for all |
| **League of Women Voters**<br>lwv.org | Nonpartisan voter education, registration, & civic engagement nationwide |
| **Southern Poverty Law Center**<br>splcenter.org | Tracks hate & extremism while advancing civil rights & justice |

## Media, Information & Protests

| Organization | Description |
| --- | --- |
| **Axios**<br>axios.com | Digital news website providing brief news articles |
| **Courier Newsroom**<br>couriernewsroom.com | Delivers accessible, values-driven local journalism to inform & engage voters |
| **Crooked Media**<br>crooked.com | Progressive media network connecting political news with meaningful civic action |
| **Daily Kos**<br>dailykos.com | Progressive news, commentary, & grassroots political organizing community |
| **FAIR**<br>**(Fairness & Accuracy in Reporting)**<br>fair.org | Media watchdog promoting accurate, ethical, accountable journalism |
| **Galvanize Action**<br>galvanizeaction.org | Builds long-term civic engagement & progressive leadership pipelines |
| **Hopium Chronicles**<br>hopiumchronicles.com | Hope-centered political commentary focused on democratic renewal |
| **Inequality Media**<br>inequalitymedia.org | Storytelling & campaigns exposing inequality & corporate influence |
| **Lincoln Project**<br>lincolnproject.us | Pro-democracy organization opposing authoritarianism & political extremism |
| **Lincoln Square Media**<br>lincolnsquare.media | Counters disinformation & strengthens democracy through fact-based media |

| Media, Information & Protests (continued) ||
|---|---|
| **Organization** | **Description** |
| **Media Matters for America** mediamatters.org | Monitors & exposes misinformation across conservative media ecosystems |
| **Meidas Touch** meidasnews.com | Pro-democracy news & commentary countering extremism & political corruption |
| **NewsGuard** newsguardtech.com | Rates news credibility & tracks online misinformation & disinformation |
| **Pod Save America** crooked.com/podcast-series/pod-save-america | Political podcast turning news analysis into civic & electoral action |
| **Pro Publica** propublica.org | Investigative journalism exposing abuses of power & threats to democracy |
| **Project Censored** projectcensored.org | Highlights underreported stories & systemic media blind spots |
| **Snopes** snopes.com | Independent fact-checking of viral claims, rumors, & misinformation |
| **The Contrarian (Substack)** substackcdn.com | Independent political commentary challenging conventional narratives |

| Political Action | |
| --- | --- |
| **Organization** | **Description** |
| **5 Calls**<br>5calls.org | Simple tools to help constituents pressure elected officials by phone |
| **Activate America**<br>activateamerica.vote | Mobilizes volunteers to support voter turnout & pro-democracy campaigns |
| **Bay Resistance**<br>bayresistance.org | Network of community organizations & unions organizing to defeat fascism in the Bay Area |
| **Corporate Accountability**<br>Corporateaccountability.org | Challenges corporate abuse & advances people-centered economic policies |
| **Indivisible**<br>indivisible.org | Grassroots movement organizing locally to defend democracy & progressive values |
| **Mobilize**<br>mobilize.us | Central hub to find volunteer actions, events, & organizing opportunities |
| **MoveOn**<br>front.moveon.org | Digital-first movement mobilizing millions for progressive change |
| **People's Union USA**<br>thepeoplesunionusa.com | Grassroots movement advocating economic justice and systemic reform |
| **The States Project**<br>statesproject.org | Supports state legislative power & helps state lawmakers govern effectively |

| Progressive Causes & Initiatives ||
| --- | --- |
| **Organization** | **Description** |
| **Americans United**<br>au.org | Protects religious freedom by defending church-state separation |
| **Brady United**<br>bradyunited.org | National advocacy organization Working to end gun violence |
| **Everytown for Gun Safety**<br>everytown.org | Research, advocacy, & grassroots action to prevent gun violence |
| **In This Together America**<br>inthistogetheramerica.org | Strengthens democracy through community-based civic participation |
| **League of Conservation Voters**<br>lcv.org | Mobilizes voters to elect climate & environmental champions |
| **March for Our Lives**<br>marchforourlives.org | Youth-led movement demanding an end to gun violence |
| **NAACP**<br>naacp.org | Oldest civil rights organization advancing racial justice and equity |

| Social Media | |
| --- | --- |
| **Organization** | **Description** |
| **Blue Sky**<br>bsky.app | Decentralized social media platform supporting open public conversation |
| **Eleanor LeCain**<br>eleanorlecain.<br>substack.come<br>(Substack) | Commentary on democracy, leadership, and civic responsibility |
| **Heather Cox Richardson (Substack)**<br>heathercoxrichardson.<br>substack.com | Historical context explaining current political and democratic challenges |
| Substack | Platform for independent writers publishing newsletters and political commentary |

| Voters, Registration, & Voting Issues | |
| --- | --- |
| **Organization** | **Description** |
| **America Votes**<br>americavotes.org | Coordinating voter registration, education, & turnout efforts |
| **Central Valley Matters**<br>centralvalleymatters.org | Local organizing focused on democracy, equity, & regional issues |
| **Commit to Democracy**<br>commit2democracy.com | Supports pro-democracy candidates & civic engagement initiatives |
| **Democracy Alliance**<br>democracyalliance.org | Network funding & strengthening progressive democracy infrastructure |
| **Electing Women Alliance**<br>electingwomenalliance.org | Supports & funds women running for elected office |

| Voters, Registration, & Voting Issues (Continued) ||
|---|---|
| **Organization** | **Description** |
| **Emily's List**<br>emilyslist.org | Elects Democratic pro-choice women to public office |
| **Fair Fight**<br>fairfight.com | Protects voting rights & combats voter suppression nationwide |
| **Flip the Vote**<br>flipthevote.org | Encourages voter turnout in key swing districts |
| **Emily's List**<br>emilyslist.org | Elects Democratic pro-choice women to public office |
| **Fair Fight**<br>fairfight.com | Protects voting rights & combats voter suppression nationwide |
| **Head Count**<br>headcount.org | Uses culture & music to register & engage young voters |
| **Leaders We Deserve**<br>leaderswedeserve.com | Backs young, values-driven candidates for public leadership |
| **Protect Democracy**<br>protectdemocracy.org | Counters authoritarian threats & defends democratic norms |
| **Rock the Vote**<br>rockthevote.org | Empowers young people to vote & participate politically |
| **Seed the Vote**<br>seedthevote.org | Trains volunteers for grassroots organizing & voter engagement |
| **States Win (Sister District)**<br>sisterdistrict.com | Supports progressive candidates in critical state legislative races |
| **Swing Left**<br>swingleft.org | Mobilizes volunteers to help Democrats win competitive elections |
| **Voters of Tomorrow**<br>votersoftomorrow.org | Building a new generation of democracy defenders |
| **Vote Forward**<br>**votefwd.org** | Letter-writing campaigns encouraging voter turnout in key races |

| Voters, Registration, & Voting Issues (Continued) | |
| --- | --- |
| **Organization** | **Description** |
| **Vote Save America** <br> votesaveamerica.com | Central hub for volunteering, donating, & election action |
| **Voter Movement Project** <br> movement.vote | Builds long-term voter engagement through relational organizing & movement building |
| **Walk the Walk** <br> walkthewalkusa.org | Relational organizing to increase voter participation through trusted networks |
| **Working America** <br> workingamerica.org | Organizes working-class voters on economic & democratic issues |

# CHAPTER 11

# Alphabetical Listing with QR Codes

| | |
|---|---|
| 5 Calls<br>5calls.org | |
| ACLU<br>aclu.org | |
| Activate America<br>activateamerica.vote | |
| America Votes<br>americavotes.org/ | |
| American Constitution Society<br>acslaw.org/ | |
| Americans United<br>au.org | |

| | |
|---|---|
| Axios<br>axios.com/ | |
| Bay Resistance<br>bayresistance.org/ | |
| Blue Sky<br>bsky.app/ | |
| Brady United<br>bradyunited.org | |
| Braver Angels<br>braverangels.org/ | |
| Brennan Center for Justice<br>brennancenter.org/ | |

| | |
|---|---|
| Campaign Legal Center<br>campaignlegal.org/ | |
| Central Valley Matters<br>centralvalleymatters.org | |
| Center for American Progress<br>americanprogress.org/ | |
| Citizens for Responsibility and<br>Ethics in Washington (CREW)<br>citizensforethics.org/ | |
| Commit to Democracy<br>commit2democracy.com/ | |

| | |
|---|---|
| Democracy Alliance<br>democracyalliance.org | |
| Democracy Docket<br>democracydocket.com/ | |
| Democracy Forward<br>democracyforward.org/ | |
| Dropsite News (Substack)<br>dropsitenews.com/ | |
| Eleanor LeCaine (Substack)<br>eleanorlecain.substack.com/ | |
| Electing Women Alliance<br>electingwomenalliance.org/ | |

| | |
|---|---|
| Election Protection<br>866-Our-Vote<br>866ourvote.org/ | |
| Emily's List<br>emilyslist.org/ | |
| Equal Citizens<br>equalcitizens.us/ | |
| Everytown for Gun Safety<br>everytown.org | |
| FAIR (Fairness & Accuracy in Reporting)<br>fair.org/ | |

| | |
|---|---|
| Fair Fight<br>fairfight.com/ | |
| FairVote (Ranked Choice Voting)<br>fairvote.org/our-reforms/ranked-choice-voting/ | |
| Flip the Vote<br>flipthevote.org/ | |
| Free Speech for People<br>freespeechforpeople.org/ | |
| Focus for Democracy<br>focus4democracy.org/ | |

| | |
|---|---|
| Galvanize Action<br>galvanizeaction.org/ | |
| Goods Unite Us<br>goodsuniteus.com/ | |
| Green is the New Black<br>greenisthenewblack.com/ | |
| Head Count<br>headcount.org/ | |
| Heather Cox Richardson<br>heathercoxrichardson.substack.com/ | |
| Hopium Chronicles<br>hopiumchronicles.com/ | |

| | |
|---|---|
| In This Together America<br>inthistogetheramerica.org | |
| Indivisible<br>indivisible.org/ | |
| Inequality Media<br>inequalitymedia.org/ | |
| Issue One<br>issueone.org/ | |
| Lawyers for Good Government<br>lawyersforgoodgovernment.org/ | |
| Leaders We Deserve<br>leaderswedeserve.com/ | |

| | |
|---|---|
| League of Conservation Voters<br>lcv.org/ | |
| League of Women Voters<br>lwv.org/ | |
| Lincoln Project<br>lincolnproject.us/ | |
| Lincoln Square Media<br>lincolnsquare.media/ | |
| Living Room Conversations<br>livingroomconversations.org | |
| March for Our Lives<br>marchforourlives.org | |

| | |
|---|---|
| Media Matters for America<br>mediamatters.org/ | |
| Meidas Touch<br>meidasnews.com/ | |
| Mobilize<br>mobilize.us/ | |
| MoveOn<br>front.moveon.org/ | |
| NAACP<br>naacp.org/ | |
| National Popular Vote<br>nationalpopularvote.com/ | |

| | |
|---|---|
| NewsGuard<br>newsguardtech.com/ | |
| Open Secrets<br>opensecrets.org/ | |
| People's Union USA<br>thepeoplesunionusa.com/ | |
| Pod Save America<br>crooked.com/podcast-<br>series/pod-save-america/ | |
| Pro Publica<br>propublica.org/ | |
| Project Censored<br>projectcensored.org/ | |

| | |
|---|---|
| Protect Democracy<br>protectdemocracy.org/ | |
| Public Citizen<br>citizen.org/ | |
| RepresentUS<br>represent.us/ | |
| Rock the Vote<br>rockthevote.org/ | |
| Seed the Vote<br>seedthevote.org/ | |

| | |
|---|---|
| Snopes<br>snopes.com/ | |
| Southern Poverty Law Center<br>splcenter.org/ | |
| States Win<br>sisterdistrict.com/ | |
| Substack<br>substack.com/home | |
| Swing Left<br>swingleft.org | |
| The Contrarian<br>substackcdn.com | |

| | |
|---|---|
| The States Project<br>statesproject.org/ | |
| Vote Forward<br>votefwd.org/ | |
| Vote Save America<br>votesaveamerica.com/ | |
| Voter Movement Project<br>movement.vote/ | |
| Voter Protection Action Committee (VPAC)<br>justice.org/ways-to-give/volunteer/vpac | |
| Voters of Tomorrow<br>votersoftomorrow.org/ | |

| Walk the Walk<br>walkthewalkusa.org/ | |
| --- | --- |
| Working America<br>workingamerica.org/ | |

# ACKNOWLEDGMENTS

This book would not have been possible without the dedication, wisdom, and hard work of many people who share a deep belief in democracy and its future. I am especially grateful to my sister, Lisa Lucks Mendel, and Helen Neville, whose tireless efforts in researching, vetting, and organizing the pro-democracy organizations featured in the book gave this work a solid foundation.

Special thanks to Alison Huetter, Lisa Lucks Mendel, and Darrell Steinberg for their invaluable editorial guidance. I am deeply appreciative as well of Darrell Steinberg and Kevin Johnson for their friendship and wise counsel in helping to shape the direction of this project.

I would also like to acknowledge Paul Davies, Jon Elliott, Joan Blades, Nathaniel Markowitz, William Westerfield, Sam Schucat, and Becca Schucat for their thoughtful assistance with research and writing. My sincere thanks go to Sariah Sizemore, Debbie Shattil, Mariah Lander, Pam Uzzell, Kelly Kirkendoll, and Susan von Seggern whose creativity brought this project to life through images, sketches, website development, social media outreach, and videos for both the book and its outreach.

This project could not have moved forward without the generous support of Howard Marks, Dan Lapporte, Dr. Michael Sands, and Karin Conn, who played an instrumental role in funding and sustaining this vision. I also want to thank Mike Isaacs, Jon Welner, Karin Conn,

Keith Stattenfield, and Doug Linney for their financial support.

Finally, my heartfelt gratitude to my publisher, Carmen Berry and Carolyn Rafferty, whose passion, commitment, and expert direction turned this idea into a published reality. To all who stood beside me—publicists, volunteers, readers, friends, and believers in a stronger democracy—thank you for your trust and conviction. Together, you helped bring *You Are the Power to Win the Future* to life.

# ABOUT THE AUTHOR

Gary Lucks, an accomplished environmental lawyer, as well as a scientist, policy adviser, professor, and Author of *You Are Not Alone: Your Roadmap to Effective Political Action*. (Available on Amazon) and founder of the Resistance Action East Bay Indivisible Group.

He has published extensively on environmental law, legislation, and policy, including co-writing a textbook and treatise chapters on environmental law. He has written policy briefing papers for California Governor Newsom, Feinstein (as a gubernatorial candidate), the former California Senate Majority Leader, and the former Insurance Commissioner.

Gary founded the Progressive Action East Bay in 2004 which raised money to help Democrats win back Congress in 2006. He later founded the Resistance Action East Bay Indivisible Group which provided the first seed money to Activate America and raised $450,000 in just three months to support Democrats in swing districts in 2020. The Indivisible group has grown to over 1,200 members.

## *Author-Led, Pro-Democracy Publishing*

Writers Integrity Network (WIN) is a pro-democracy publishing house created to mobilize writers whose books can unite and equip Americans to confront the current assault on American democracy. WIN was founded by publishing professionals Carolyn Rafferty and Carmen Renee Berry, a New York Times bestselling author.

### Truth Has Power. We wield it.

Writers are democracy's first line of defense. We believe the pen, wielded with integrity, can shift culture, expose injustice, and hold power accountable.

### Authors Lead. Democracy Follows.

When writers organize, movements ignite. We champion author-led action because storytellers don't just reflect the times — they change them.

### Silence Is Not an Option.

This moment demands voices, not observers. We call every writer to show up, speak out, and use their platform in service of a just and democratic society. Write like it matters — because it does.

WIN is accepting manuscripts and book ideas from aspiring and published authors. Please visit our website and contact us: www.writersintegritynetwork.com

### *YOU ARE NOT ALONE*
### *Your Roadmap to Effective Political Action*
### **Gary Lucks**

If America is to survive…we need a new and resilient political movement, born of progressivism and patriotism. Gary Lucks shows what works for a better future.
*--Joel Makower, Chairman, Trellis Group and the author of The Grand New Strategy*

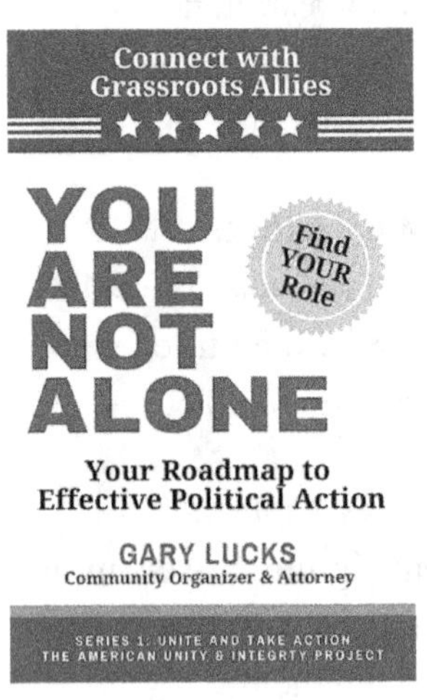


In a time when political noise can feel overwhelming, Gary Lucks offers a clear voice of hope and direction. *You Are Not Alone* is a guide for anyone who feels discouraged, anxious, or powerless in the face of today's political chaos. Instead of watching from the sidelines, Gary shows you how to step into meaningful action.

This book introduces you to a nationwide movement of citizens committed to protecting democracy and resisting authoritarian threats. Along the way, you'll find practical tools for getting involved, stories of grassroots success, and the reassurance that you are not in this fight by yourself.

### *THE COST OF DOING NOTHING*
### *Is a Price We Cannot Pay*
### Rabbi Henry Jay Karp

Adolf Hitler destroyed the German democracy in a mere fifty-three days. Our democracy is also falling into authoritarianism, as Rabbi Karp predicted in this book, published in early 2025.

Rabbi Henry Jay Karp is a professor at St. Ambrose University in Davenport, Iowa, teaching courses in Jewish history, with an emphasis on the Holocaust

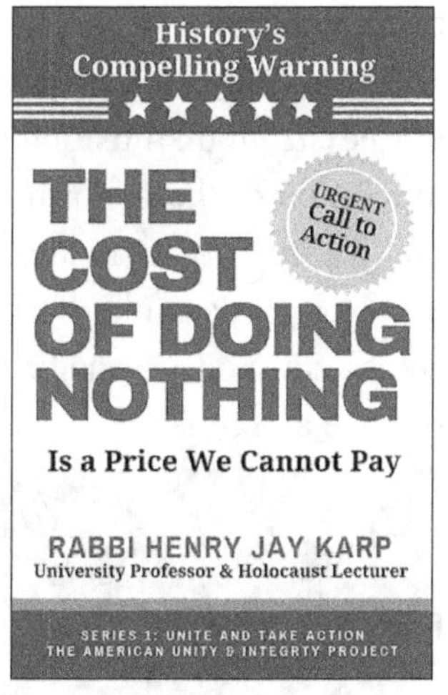


*The Cost of Doing Nothing* is fascinating, convincing, and alarming, as it exposes how clearly the Trump administration's swift dive to authoritarianism reflects Hitler's rise to power and the subsequent Holocaust. Not to be dismissed as overreach, this informed and calmly presented position is alert to the most recent deprivations of democracy coming from the White House.
*-- Alan Garfield, Professor Emeritus, University of Dubuque.*

## *ONE BETRAYAL TOO MANY*
### *Why I Left MAGA*
### Rich Logis

*This book is a public apology. I am profoundly sorry for the damage I caused during the seven years I was in the MAGA movement. I contributed to the assault on our democracy. I exacerbated the harm caused to others in MAGA. Now I am holding myself accountable by working to make amends.* --Rich Logis

So begins *One Betrayal Too Many, Why I Left MAGA* by Rich Logis, former MAGA activist, podcaster, and commentator.

Logis takes us on a deeply personal and agonizing journey from disillusionment with the MAGA movement to founder of the nonprofit *Leaving MAGA*. *One Betrayal Too Many* attracts readers across political lines because it's not a partisan manifesto. It is a human story about how democracy erodes—and how it can be defended—one conscience at a time.

As millions of Americans remain trapped inside a movement fueled by fear, grievance, and misinformation, *One Betrayal Too Many* offers something rare: a bridge. It speaks directly to those who feel uneasy but are afraid to leave—and to those who want to help loved ones without pushing them further away.

Unlike books written about MAGA from the outside, *One Betrayal Too Many* is written from within. Logis does not present himself as a victim or hero. Instead, he offers a rare and unsparing act of accountability: a public apology for the role he played in spreading disinformation, dehumanization, and fear—and a blueprint for how people can leave extremist movements without losing their dignity, identity, or community.

The book opens with a foreword by former Republican Congressman Adam Kinzinger, who places Logis's personal story within the larger fight to preserve constitutional democracy.

Rich Logis is the founder and CEO of Leaving MAGA. He has dedicated his life to undoing the political damage he caused during his seven years as a devoted MAGA activist. He is especially proud of the growing number of testimonials Leaving MAGA has published of others who have left MAGA, and of the organization's support group for people with friends and family in the movement.

Rich has a large social media following, frequently speaks around the country, and has been featured on CNN, MS NOW, and many other outlets, including major foreign newspapers and TV programs. He lives in Florida with his wife and two daughters.

### *THE AMERICAN OATH PROJECT*
### Protecting the Backbone of Democracy
### Kevin K. Johnson

The American Oath Project was created by experienced mediator and California civil trial and appellate lawyer Kevin K. Johnson, JD, and seeks to educate, unify, and empower the American people to take legal and civic action, guided by the spirit and principles of the United States Constitution. This book proposes the pursuit of civil lawsuits designed to end Mr. Trump's Presidential Employment Contract for both premeditated and ongoing, cumulative and coordinated breaches of the Presidential Oath of Office, and for committing "fraud in the inducement" by lying when he took the Oath.

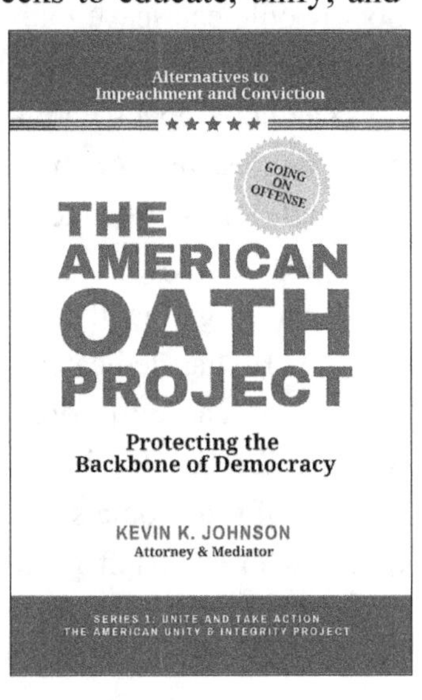


Kevin K. Johnson, MA, JD, is a civil trial and appellate lawyer and mediator in California who has negotiated with or litigated against major oil companies, national insurance carriers, regional and local governments, the State of California, and the U.S. Government. He has represented Fortune 500 Companies, served on non-profit boards, and is regularly active in organizing voter turnout efforts.

## *BECAUSE WE ARE AMERICANS*
### We Are Pro-Democracy
### Carmen Renee Berry & Carolyn Rafferty

Does being an American mean that you believe in democracy? Not anymore. Our country is spiraling into authoritarianism, and some Americans are cheering.

*Because We Are Americans* is more than just a book-- it's a call to action for every American—to raise your voice, join a broad coalition, and make a difference through creative, nonviolent activism through a social media campaign.

Carmen Renee Berry MSW, New York Times bestselling author, has written multiple books on self-care and preventing burnout. Her books have been published by houses including HarperCollins, Simon & Schuster, Penguin, and Thomas Nelson.

Carolyn Rafferty has over 40 years of experience in professional media production and distribution. She is co-founder of Berry Powell Press and Writers Integrity Network. She holds a Master's Degree in Intercultural Studies and has applied that skill set to multiple overseas adventures.